Table of Contents

The Urgency of Mental Health in Education

Creating Supportive Learning Environments for Students and Staff

Percy Chris Kpodo

Published by Wordsculpt Consult
First Edition: 2024

Dedication

To Mrs. Agnes Adzoa Kpodo,

Your unwavering love and support have provided the perfect environment for my educational journey and mental well-being. This book is dedicated to you, my beloved mother, for creating that nurturing space where I could thrive, both academically and personally. Your strength, compassion, and encouragement have been the foundation of my success.

Acknowledgements

This book is the result of countless hours of research, reflection, and collaboration. I am deeply grateful to everyone who contributed to its creation.

First and foremost, I would like to thank my family for their unwavering support and encouragement. Your belief in me has been the foundation upon which this work is built.

A special thank you to Karios Impact Ventures and Wordsculpt Consult for their meticulous attention to detail and thoughtful guidance throughout the editing and publication process.

I am also grateful to the many educators, administrators, and policymakers who shared their experiences and perspectives. Your stories and insights are the heart of this book, and I am honored to include them.

Lastly, thank you to my readers. Your quest for knowledge and your commitment to improving education are what drive this work. I hope this book serves as a valuable resource on your journey of transformation and growth.

Introduction

The Urgency of Mental Health in Education

In recent years, the issue of mental health has gained significant attention, particularly within the educational sector. The COVID-19 pandemic has further magnified the mental health crisis, exposing vulnerabilities in how schools and universities support the psychological wellbeing of their students and staff. The closure of schools, the shift to online learning, and the uncertainty about the future have collectively contributed to increased levels of anxiety, depression, and stress among students and educators alike (Golberstein, Wen, & Miller, 2020). This book, "Mental Health and Wellbeing in Education," seeks to address these urgent concerns by providing a comprehensive guide for educators, administrators, parents, and policymakers to foster a supportive environment conducive to mental health and wellbeing.

Mental health issues among students are not a new phenomenon, but their prevalence and impact have surged dramatically. According to the World Health Organization (WHO), one in six children and adolescents aged 10-19 years old suffers from a mental disorder, and half of all mental illnesses begin by the age of 14 (WHO, 2021). These statistics underscore the critical need for early identification and intervention in the educational setting. Schools are in a unique position to play a pivotal role in promoting mental health, yet many are ill-equipped to do so effectively.

The pandemic has exacerbated existing mental health issues and created new challenges. Research by Golberstein, Wen, and Miller (2020) indicates a significant rise in anxiety and depression symptoms among students due to the pandemic. The disruption of routines, social isolation, and the shift to remote learning have all contributed to this increase. The stress is not limited to students; educators have also faced unprecedented pressures. Balancing remote teaching, dealing with technological challenges, and managing their own health concerns have left many teachers feeling overwhelmed and burnt out (Kim & Asbury, 2020).

Schools have always been more than just places of academic learning; they are also crucial social environments where children develop emotionally and socially. By integrating mental health support into the fabric of the school system, we can create a nurturing environment that helps students thrive. This involves not just recognizing and addressing mental health issues, but also fostering resilience and emotional intelligence.

Mental health encompasses emotional, psychological, and social well-being. It affects how individuals think, feel, and act, influencing their ability to handle stress, relate to others, and make choices. In the educational context, mental health is closely linked to academic performance, attendance, and overall school climate (Kessler et al., 2005). Poor mental health can lead to academic difficulties, absenteeism, and behavioural problems, creating a cycle that can be difficult to break.

Early identification of mental health issues is crucial. Educators, who interact with students on a daily basis, are often the first to notice changes in behaviour that may indicate a mental health problem. Training teachers to recognize the signs and symptoms of common mental health disorders can significantly impact students' lives. Tools such as the Strengths and Difficulties Questionnaire (SDQ) and the Patient Health Questionnaire (PHQ-9) can aid in early detection (Goodman, 2001; Kroenke, Spitzer, & Williams, 2001).

There is a well-documented link between mental health and academic performance. Students with untreated mental health issues often struggle academically. Anxiety, depression, and attention disorders can impair concentration, memory, and energy levels, making it difficult for students to perform well in school (Reupert et al., 2012). Conversely, a positive school environment that supports mental health can enhance academic outcomes. Implementing strategies to support mental health can lead to improved attendance, higher grades, and better overall school engagement.

A supportive school environment is one where students feel safe, valued, and understood. This involves creating a culture that prioritizes mental health, implementing anti-bullying programs, and encouraging open conversations about mental health. Social and Emotional Learning (SEL) programs are effective in teaching students how to manage their emotions, set goals, show empathy for others, and maintain positive relationships (Durlak et al., 2011). These skills are not only crucial for mental health but also for academic and life success.

Parents and guardians play a critical role in supporting their children's mental health. Engaging parents in school mental health initiatives can create a stronger support system for students. Communication between parents and teachers is vital for identifying and addressing mental health issues early. Schools can offer resources and workshops to help parents understand mental health and how they can support their children at home (Fazel et al., 2014).

Educators need ongoing professional development to effectively support student mental health. Training in mental health literacy can equip teachers with the knowledge and skills to identify and respond to mental health issues. Additionally, educators need strategies for self-care to manage their own stress and prevent burnout. Building resilience among educators is essential for creating a stable and supportive learning environment (Jennings & Greenberg, 2009).

Successful school-based mental health programs require careful planning and collaboration with mental health professionals. These programs should be integrated into the school's existing framework and tailored to meet the specific needs of the student population. Funding and sustainability are also critical considerations. Ongoing evaluation is necessary to measure the program's impact and make necessary adjustments (Weist et al., 2014).

Schools must be prepared to handle mental health crises. Developing a crisis response plan ensures that staff know how to respond effectively to emergencies. Post-crisis support is also important to help students and staff recover and build resilience. Collaborating with community resources can provide additional support and services during a crisis (Brock et al., 2009).

Technology offers new opportunities for supporting mental health in education. Digital tools and apps can provide students with access to mental health resources and support. Telehealth services can offer remote counselling, making it easier for students to get help when needed. Social media can also play a role in raising awareness and reducing the stigma associated with mental health issues (Naslund, Aschbrenner, Marsch, & Bartels, 2016).

Advocacy is crucial for driving systemic change. Educators, parents, and students can work together to advocate for policies that support mental health in schools. Understanding current policies and their impact can help identify areas for improvement. Learning from international perspectives can also provide valuable insights and strategies for advocacy (Kutcher & Wei, 2013).

The mental health and wellbeing of students and educators are critical components of a successful education system. By understanding the challenges and implementing effective strategies, we can create a supportive environment that promotes mental health and academic success. This book provides a comprehensive guide to help schools, educators, parents, and policymakers address mental health issues and foster a culture of wellbeing. Together, we can make a difference in the lives of students and educators around the world.

Chapter 1

Understanding Mental Health in Education

1.1 Definition and Importance of Mental Health

Mental health, often misunderstood and stigmatized, is a critical aspect of overall well-being that encompasses emotional, psychological, and social well-being. It influences how individuals think, feel, and act, as well as how they handle stress, relate to others, and make choices. In the educational context, mental health is particularly significant as it directly impacts students' learning, behaviour, and overall school experience.

Definition of Mental Health

Mental health can be defined as a state of well-being in which an individual realizes their own abilities, can cope with the normal stresses of life, can work productively, and is able to make a contribution to their community (World Health Organization, 2004). This definition highlights the multifaceted nature of mental health, encompassing emotional stability, cognitive functioning, and social skills.

Mental health is not merely the absence of mental illness but a positive state of mental functioning. According to the American Psychiatric Association (2013), good mental health is characterized by a sense of well-being, self-efficacy, autonomy, competence, and the ability to recognize and realize emotional and intellectual potential. This holistic view underscores the importance of mental health as a dynamic and integral part of life.

Importance of Mental Health in Education

Impact on Academic Performance

The connection between mental health and academic performance is well-documented. Students with good mental health are more likely to attend school regularly, engage in the classroom, and achieve better academic outcomes (Kessler et al., 2005). Conversely, mental health issues such as anxiety, depression, and attention disorders can hinder concentration, reduce energy levels, and impair cognitive functions, leading to lower academic achievement and increased absenteeism (Reupert et al., 2012).

For example, a study by Durlak et al. (2011) found that social and emotional learning (SEL) programs, which aim to improve mental health, resulted in significantly improved academic performance. Students participating in SEL programs showed an average gain of 11 percentile points in academic achievement compared to their peers who did not participate in such programs. This demonstrates the profound impact that addressing mental health can have on students' educational outcomes.

Social and Emotional Development

Mental health is also crucial for students' social and emotional development. Schools are social environments where children learn to interact with peers, develop relationships, and build social skills. Mental health problems can interfere with these processes, leading to social withdrawal, difficulties in peer relationships, and increased risk of bullying (Fazel et al., 2014).

Promoting mental health in schools helps students develop resilience, emotional regulation, and coping strategies. These skills are essential for navigating the complexities of adolescence and adulthood. Programs that focus on social and emotional learning help students manage their emotions, set positive goals, show empathy for others, and maintain healthy relationships, all of which contribute to a supportive and inclusive school environment (Durlak et al., 2011).

Behaviour and Discipline

Students' mental health significantly influences their behaviour and discipline in school. Mental health issues such as conduct disorders, anxiety, and depression can manifest as disruptive behaviour, non-compliance, or aggression, challenging teachers and disrupting the learning environment (Reinke et al., 2011). Addressing these issues through mental health support and interventions can lead to improved behaviour, fewer disciplinary actions, and a more positive classroom atmosphere.

Implementing comprehensive mental health programs can reduce the incidence of behavioural problems. For instance, the Positive Behavioural Interventions and Supports (PBIS) framework has been shown to improve student behaviour and create a more positive school climate. PBIS emphasizes proactive strategies for defining, teaching, and supporting appropriate student behaviours to create a positive school environment (Sugai & Horner, 2002).

Long-term Outcomes

The importance of mental health extends beyond the immediate school years. Mental health issues that emerge in childhood and adolescence can have long-term consequences for individuals' health, social relationships, and economic productivity. Early intervention and support can prevent the escalation of mental health problems and promote positive outcomes in adulthood (Kessler et al., 2005).

Addressing mental health in schools also contributes to the development of a healthier, more productive society. Students who receive mental health support are more likely to graduate, pursue higher education, and contribute positively to their communities. This highlights the broader societal benefits of prioritizing mental health in education.

Barriers to Addressing Mental Health in Schools

Despite the clear importance of mental health in education, there are several barriers to effectively addressing this issue in schools. Stigma and misconceptions about mental health often prevent students, parents, and educators from seeking help. Additionally, many schools lack the resources and trained personnel to provide adequate mental health support (Fazel et al., 2014).

Stigma remains a significant barrier, leading to underreporting and reluctance to seek help. Educating the school community about mental health and creating a culture of acceptance and support are crucial steps in overcoming this barrier. Schools need to prioritize mental health education and awareness to reduce stigma and encourage open conversations about mental health.

Resource constraints also pose a challenge. Many schools do not have access to school counsellors, psychologists, or social workers who can provide mental health support. Policymakers and educational leaders must advocate for increased funding and resources to ensure that all students have access to the mental health services they need.

1.2 Historical Perspectives on Mental Health in Schools

Understanding the historical context of mental health in education provides essential insights into the evolution of support systems and practices within schools. This journey reflects societal shifts, scientific advancements, and changes in educational philosophy, revealing how mental health has become integral to the educational landscape.

Early 20th Century: The Foundations of School Psychology

The early 1900s marked the beginning of school psychology, with pioneers like Lightner Witmer laying the groundwork. Witmer's establishment of the first child guidance clinic in 1896 highlighted the need for psychological services in schools. His approach focused on diagnosing and treating learning and behavioural problems, setting the stage for integrating psychological services into education (Witmer, 1909).

During this period, mental health in schools was primarily concerned with identifying and managing "problem" children to enhance their academic performance. The tools were basic, relying on observational assessments rather than the sophisticated diagnostics we use today. This early work laid a crucial foundation, but mental health support remained limited in scope and understanding.

Mid-20th Century: Expansion and Legislation

The mid-20th century saw significant strides with the expansion of psychological services in schools. Following World War II, there was a growing awareness of the psychological impact of trauma on children. This era saw the development of standardized tests and more refined psychological assessments, which helped in better identifying mental health issues among students.

In 1975, the Education for All Handicapped Children Act (now IDEA) was enacted, mandating that schools provide appropriate services to students with disabilities, including those with emotional and behavioural disorders. This legislation was a landmark in promoting inclusive education, ensuring that children with mental health challenges received necessary support within the school system.

Late 20th Century: A Shift Towards Holistic Approaches

By the late 20th century, the focus of mental health in schools broadened to include overall psychological well-being, not just severe disorders. Comprehensive school health programs emerged, integrating mental health with other health initiatives. The CDC's Coordinated School Health Program, introduced in the 1980s, emphasized a holistic approach, combining mental health, nutrition, physical education, and safety to promote student health and well-being.

This period also saw the rise of evidence-based programs aimed at preventing mental health issues and promoting resilience among students. Programs like Positive Behavioural Interventions and Supports (PBIS) and Social and Emotional Learning (SEL) became prominent. PBIS focused on proactive strategies to define, teach, and support positive behaviours, while SEL programs equipped students with critical skills for emotional regulation, empathy, and relationship-building.

Early 21st Century: Prevention and Early Intervention

The early 21st century brought a strong emphasis on prevention and early intervention. Research increasingly highlighted the benefits of early support in improving long-term outcomes for children with mental health issues. Schools began adopting more structured frameworks, such as multi-tiered systems of support (MTSS), which provided varying levels of intervention based on student needs.

The rise of technology also played a significant role, with online resources and digital tools making mental health information more accessible. Telehealth services and mental health apps became valuable assets, especially in remote or underserved areas. These innovations have broadened the scope of mental health support, making it more inclusive and readily available to those who need it most.

Contemporary Trends and Future Directions

Today, mental health in schools continues to evolve with a focus on creating supportive environments that prioritize the well-being of all students. The COVID-19 pandemic has underscored the critical need for robust mental health support, pushing schools to adopt trauma-informed care and resilience-building strategies. This shift has highlighted the importance of not just addressing mental health issues but also fostering a culture of mental wellness.

Looking ahead, the integration of mental health in education is expected to deepen, with a growing emphasis on collaboration among educators, mental health professionals, and families. Schools are increasingly adopting data-driven approaches to tailor interventions to individual student needs, ensuring that mental health support is both effective and sustainable.

1.3 Current Trends and Statistics

In recent years, the focus on mental health within the educational sector has grown exponentially. This shift has been driven by a combination of increased awareness, evolving societal attitudes, and a growing body of research highlighting the critical role of mental health in academic success and overall well-being. Understanding the current trends and statistics is essential for grasping the scope of mental health issues in schools and the efforts being made to address them.

Rising Prevalence of Mental Health Issues

Recent studies indicate a significant increase in mental health issues among children and adolescents. According to the World Health Organization (2021), one in seven 10–19-year-olds experiences a mental disorder, with depression and anxiety being the most common. These disorders can profoundly affect a student's ability to learn, engage socially, and maintain a healthy school-life balance.

The National Institute of Mental Health (NIMH) reports that approximately 31.9% of adolescents in the United States have an anxiety disorder, with the prevalence higher in females than males (Merikangas et al., 2010). Similarly, the prevalence of major depressive episodes in adolescents has increased from 8.7% in 2005 to 13.3% in 2017 (Mojtabai, Olfson, & Han, 2016). This rising trend underscores the urgent need for effective mental health interventions in schools.

Impact of the COVID-19 Pandemic

The COVID-19 pandemic has further exacerbated mental health challenges among students. The sudden shift to remote learning, social isolation, and uncertainty about the future have all contributed to increased levels of stress, anxiety, and depression. A study by the Centres for Disease Control and Prevention (CDC) found that mental health-related emergency department visits increased by 24% for children aged 5-11 and by 31% for adolescents aged 12-17 during the pandemic (Leeb et al., 2020).

These findings highlight the profound impact of the pandemic on student mental health and underscore the importance of integrating mental health support into the educational framework to help students cope with the ongoing challenges.

School-Based Mental Health Services

Recognizing the growing mental health needs of students, schools are increasingly incorporating mental health services into their support systems. Approximately 70-80% of children and adolescents who receive mental health services access them through school (Farmer et al., 2003). This trend is driven by the recognition that schools are uniquely positioned to provide accessible mental health support.

Schools are adopting a variety of models to deliver mental health services, including:

1. **School Counsellors and Psychologists**: Many schools employ counsellors and psychologists who provide individual and group therapy, crisis intervention, and mental health education. The American School Counsellor Association (ASCA) recommends a ratio of one counsellor per 250 students to effectively meet students' needs.

2. **School-Based Health Centres (SBHCs)**: SBHCs offer comprehensive health services, including mental health care, directly on school grounds. These centres provide convenient access to care, reducing barriers such as transportation and cost. Research shows that SBHCs are associated with improved mental health outcomes and academic performance (Guo et al., 2008).

3. **Multi-Tiered Systems of Support (MTSS)**: MTSS frameworks, including Positive Behavioural Interventions and Supports (PBIS) and Social and Emotional Learning (SEL) programs, provide a structured approach to supporting student mental health. These systems offer varying levels of intervention based on students' needs, from universal

prevention strategies to targeted and intensive supports.

The Role of Technology

Technology is playing an increasingly important role in supporting student mental health. Digital tools and platforms offer new avenues for mental health education, assessment, and intervention. For example:

1. **Telehealth**: Telehealth services provide remote access to mental health care, making it easier for students in underserved or rural areas to receive support. Telehealth has become particularly valuable during the COVID-19 pandemic, enabling continuity of care despite social distancing measures.

2. **Mental Health Apps**: Numerous apps offer resources for managing stress, anxiety, and other mental health issues. Apps like Headspace and Calm provide mindfulness and relaxation exercises, while platforms like Mood Kit offer cognitive-behavioural therapy (CBT) tools.

3. **Online Counselling Services**: Platforms like Better Help and Talk space connect students with licensed therapists for virtual counselling sessions. These services offer flexibility and anonymity, which can be particularly appealing to adolescents.

Emphasis on Social and Emotional Learning (SEL)

Social and Emotional Learning (SEL) has become a cornerstone of mental health promotion in schools. SEL programs teach students critical skills for managing emotions, setting goals, showing empathy, maintaining positive relationships, and making responsible decisions. Research shows that SEL programs can significantly improve students' mental health, behaviour, and academic performance (Durlak et al., 2011).

Programs such as the Collaborative for Academic, Social, and Emotional Learning (CASEL) provide frameworks and resources for implementing SEL in schools. CASEL's research indicates that students who participate in SEL programs show an 11% improvement in academic performance, as well as reductions in anxiety, depression, and behavioural problems.

Mental Health Policy and Advocacy

Policy and advocacy efforts are crucial for sustaining and expanding mental health services in schools. Legislative measures such as the Mental Health in Schools Act in the United States aim to increase funding for school-based mental health programs and services. Advocacy organizations like the National Alliance on Mental Illness (NAMI) work to raise awareness and support policies that promote mental health in educational settings.

Internationally, initiatives like the World Health Organization's Mental Health Action Plan 2013-2020 emphasize the importance of integrating mental health services into schools as part of a broader strategy to improve mental health outcomes globally.

1.4 The Impact of the Pandemic on Student and Staff Mental Health

The COVID-19 pandemic has had a profound impact on every aspect of life, including education. The abrupt transition to remote learning, prolonged social isolation, and the pervasive sense of uncertainty have significantly affected the mental health of both students and staff. This section explores the various ways in which the pandemic has influenced mental health in educational settings, drawing on current research and statistics.

Impact on Students

Increased Anxiety and Depression

The pandemic has led to a marked increase in anxiety and depression among students. According to a study by the Centres for Disease Control and Prevention (CDC), the proportion of mental health-related emergency department visits increased by 24% for children aged 5-11 and by 31% for those aged 12-17 during the pandemic (Leeb et al., 2020). The disruption of daily routines, fears about the virus, and the challenges of remote learning have contributed to heightened levels of stress and anxiety.

In addition, a survey conducted by the American Psychological Association (APA) found that more than 70% of teenagers reported experiencing significant stress related to the pandemic, with concerns about academic performance, social isolation, and family health being the primary stressors (APA, 2020).

Social Isolation and Loneliness

The shift to online learning and the closure of schools have led to significant social isolation for many students. Social interactions are a crucial part of adolescent development, and the lack of face-to-face contact with peers has led to feelings of loneliness and isolation. A study published in the *Journal of the American Academy of Child & Adolescent Psychiatry* found that social isolation during the pandemic was associated with increased rates of depression and anxiety among adolescents (Loades et al., 2020).

Academic Stress and Uncertainty

The transition to remote learning presented numerous challenges, including technological issues, lack of access to reliable internet, and difficulties in adapting to new modes of instruction. These challenges exacerbated academic stress for many students. According to research by the EdWeek Research Centre, approximately 65% of students reported increased stress levels due to difficulties with online learning platforms and maintaining academic performance (EdWeek Research Center, 2020).

Furthermore, the uncertainty surrounding standardized testing, college admissions, and future educational prospects added to the stress. The disruption of traditional academic milestones, such as graduations and proms, also contributed to a sense of loss and disappointment.

Impact on Staff

Teacher Burnout and Stress

Teachers have faced unprecedented challenges during the pandemic. The rapid transition to online teaching required significant adjustments, often with little training or support. Many educators had to navigate new technologies, redesign curricula for remote delivery, and manage their own health concerns, all while supporting their students' learning and well-being.

A survey by the National Education Association (NEA) found that 28% of teachers reported that the pandemic had made them more likely to leave the teaching profession or retire early (NEA, 2020). The increased workload, combined with the stress of balancing professional and personal responsibilities, has led to high levels of burnout and fatigue among educators.

Emotional Toll and Mental Health Challenges

The emotional toll of the pandemic on teachers has been significant. Many educators have reported feelings of anxiety, depression, and helplessness. A study published in the *Journal of Educational Psychology* found that teachers experienced increased levels of stress and anxiety during the pandemic, particularly those who felt unprepared for online teaching and those who lacked support from their schools (Pressley, 2021).

Teachers also faced the challenge of supporting their students' mental health while managing their own. The constant need to be emotionally available for students, coupled with their own personal and family health concerns, has exacerbated mental health issues among educators.

Adaptation and Resilience

Despite these challenges, many educators have demonstrated remarkable resilience and adaptability. Teachers have found innovative ways to engage students, build virtual communities, and provide support. Professional development and peer support networks have played a crucial role in helping teachers navigate these challenging times.

Schools that prioritized teacher well-being and provided adequate resources and support were better able to maintain a positive school climate and support both staff and students effectively. This highlights the importance of institutional support in fostering resilience among educators.

Broader Implications and Long-Term Effects

Disparities in Mental Health Impact

The impact of the pandemic on mental health has not been uniform across all student and staff populations. Vulnerable groups, including students from low-income families, students with disabilities, and students of color, have faced greater challenges. These groups often had less access to mental health resources, technology, and safe learning environments, exacerbating pre-existing disparities in mental health and educational outcomes (García & Weiss, 2020).

Long-Term Mental Health Implications

The long-term mental health implications of the pandemic are still unfolding. Prolonged exposure to stress and trauma can have lasting effects on both students and educators. Schools will need to continue prioritizing mental health support and interventions to address these ongoing challenges.

The pandemic has also highlighted the importance of integrating mental health into the broader educational framework. Schools that have built robust mental health support systems are better equipped to handle such crises and support their communities. Moving forward, there is a critical need to ensure that mental health remains a central focus in educational policies and practices.

1.5 The Role of Schools in Promoting Mental Health

Schools play a pivotal role in promoting mental health and well-being among students. Given that children and adolescents spend a significant portion of their lives in school, these institutions are uniquely positioned to influence their mental health positively. This section explores how schools can create supportive environments, implement effective mental health programs, and foster a culture that prioritizes emotional well-being.

Creating a Supportive Environment

Building a Positive School Climate

A positive school climate is essential for promoting mental health. It involves creating an environment where students feel safe, respected, and valued. Research indicates that students in schools with a positive climate are more likely to experience better mental health and academic outcomes (Thapa, Cohen, Guffey, & Higgins-D'Alessandro, 2013). Elements of a positive school climate include:

- **Respectful Relationships**: Encouraging respectful and supportive relationships among students and between students and staff can help create a sense of belonging.

- **Safety and Security**: Ensuring physical and emotional safety in school reduces stress and anxiety.
- **Inclusive Practices**: Promoting inclusivity and diversity helps all students feel accepted and reduces the incidence of bullying and discrimination.

Social and Emotional Learning (SEL)

Social and Emotional Learning (SEL) programs are fundamental in promoting mental health. SEL focuses on developing students' skills in managing emotions, setting goals, establishing positive relationships, and making responsible decisions. Implementing SEL programs can lead to improvements in students' mental health, social behaviour, and academic performance (Durlak et al., 2011). Key components of SEL include:

- **Self-Awareness**: Helping students understand their emotions and values.
- **Self-Management**: Teaching strategies for regulating emotions and behaviours.
- **Social Awareness**: Promoting empathy and understanding of others.
- **Relationship Skills**: Developing communication and conflict resolution skills.
- **Responsible Decision-Making**: Encouraging thoughtful and ethical choices.

Implementing Mental Health Programs
School-Based Mental Health Services

Integrating mental health services within schools is crucial for early identification and intervention. School-based mental health services can include counselling, psychological services, and social work. These services provide accessible support for students who may not otherwise have access to mental health care. According to the National Association of School Psychologists (NASP), schools should aim for a ratio of one school psychologist per 500-700 students to adequately address mental health needs (NASP, 2016).

Multi-Tiered Systems of Support (MTSS)

Multi-Tiered Systems of Support (MTSS) is an evidence-based framework that provides varying levels of support based on student needs. MTSS includes:

- **Tier 1: Universal Interventions**: School-wide programs that promote mental health for all students, such as SEL and positive behaviour interventions.
- **Tier 2: Targeted Interventions**: Support for students identified as at risk for mental health issues, such as small group counselling.
- **Tier 3: Intensive Interventions**: Individualized support for students with significant mental health needs, including one-on-one therapy.

MTSS helps schools efficiently allocate resources and ensure that all students receive the appropriate level of support.

Collaboration with Community Resources

Schools can enhance their mental health services by collaborating with community organizations and mental health professionals. Partnerships with local health agencies, non-profits, and mental health clinics can provide additional resources and expertise. For example, school-based health centres (SBHCs) often collaborate with community health providers to offer comprehensive services, including mental health care (Guo et al., 2008).

Fostering a Mental Health-Friendly Culture

Reducing Stigma

One of the significant barriers to seeking mental health support is stigma. Schools can play a critical role in reducing stigma by fostering an open and accepting culture. This can be achieved through:

- **Mental Health Education**: Incorporating mental health

education into the curriculum helps students understand and normalize mental health issues.

- **Awareness Campaigns**: School-wide campaigns can raise awareness about mental health and encourage students to seek help.
- **Peer Support Programs**: Training students to support their peers can create a more supportive school community.

Staff Training and Professional Development

Teachers and school staff are often the first to notice changes in students' behaviour and well-being. Providing staff with training in mental health awareness and intervention equips them to respond effectively. Professional development programs can include:

- **Recognizing Signs of Mental Health Issues**: Training on identifying symptoms of common mental health disorders.
- **Crisis Intervention**: Preparing staff to handle mental health emergencies.
- **Self-Care Strategies**: Ensuring that staff also prioritize their own mental health and well-being.

Family and Community Engagement

Engaging families and the wider community is essential for promoting mental health. Schools can:

- **Provide Resources and Workshops**: Offer information and training sessions for parents on supporting their children's mental health.
- **Encourage Parental Involvement**: Foster strong partnerships between parents and schools to support students' mental health.
- **Collaborate with Community Leaders**: Work with local leaders to address broader social determinants of mental health, such as poverty and violence.

Measuring and Evaluating Impact

To ensure the effectiveness of mental health programs, schools must regularly assess and evaluate their impact. This involves:

- **Data Collection**: Gathering data on student mental health outcomes, program participation, and satisfaction.
- **Continuous Improvement**: Using data to refine and improve mental health initiatives.
- **Reporting and Accountability**: Sharing outcomes with stakeholders, including students, parents, staff, and the community.

Schools have a critical role in promoting mental health and well-being. By creating a supportive environment, implementing comprehensive mental health programs, and fostering a culture that prioritizes emotional well-being, schools can significantly impact the mental health of their students and staff. As educational institutions continue to evolve, integrating mental health into the core mission of schools will be essential for fostering resilient, healthy, and successful students.

Chapter 2

Identifying Mental Health Issues in Students

Identifying mental health issues in students is a critical step in providing timely and effective support. Early detection can prevent the escalation of problems and improve outcomes for students. This chapter explores common mental health disorders in youth, signs and symptoms to watch for, screening and assessment tools, the role of teachers and staff in identification, and case studies of early identification and intervention.

2.1 Common Mental Health Disorders in Youth

Anxiety Disorders

Anxiety disorders are among the most common mental health issues affecting children and adolescents. These disorders can manifest as generalized anxiety disorder (GAD), panic disorder, social anxiety disorder, and specific phobias. Symptoms often include excessive worry, restlessness, fatigue, difficulty concentrating, and physical symptoms such as headaches and stomach-aches.

Depression

Depression in youth is characterized by persistent feelings of sadness, irritability, and loss of interest in activities. Other symptoms may include changes in appetite or weight, sleep disturbances, fatigue, feelings of worthlessness or guilt, and thoughts of death or suicide. The prevalence of depression in adolescents has been increasing, with significant impacts on academic performance and social interactions (Mojtabai, Olfson, & Han, 2016).

Attention-Deficit/Hyperactivity Disorder (ADHD)

ADHD is marked by patterns of inattention, hyperactivity, and impulsivity that interfere with functioning or development. Symptoms include difficulty sustaining attention, frequent fidgeting, excessive talking, and trouble waiting turns. ADHD can affect academic performance and social relationships, making early identification and intervention crucial.

Autism Spectrum Disorder (ASD)

ASD is a developmental disorder characterized by challenges with social interaction, communication, and repetitive behaviours. Early signs of ASD include delayed speech development, lack of interest in peer interactions, and unusual responses to sensory experiences. Early diagnosis and intervention can significantly improve outcomes for children with ASD.

Conduct Disorders

Conduct disorders involve a pattern of behaviour that violates the rights of others or major societal norms. Symptoms include aggression toward people and animals, destruction of property, deceitfulness or theft, and serious violations of rules. Early intervention is essential to prevent the progression to more severe behavioural problems.

2.2 Signs and Symptoms of Mental Health Problems

Recognizing the signs and symptoms of mental health issues is the first step in providing help. Teachers, parents, and peers play a crucial role in identifying these symptoms, which may vary depending on the age and development of the child. Common signs include:

- **Changes in Behaviour**: Sudden or gradual changes in behaviour, such as withdrawal from social interactions, aggressive behaviour, or extreme mood swings.
- **Academic Decline**: A noticeable drop in academic performance, frequent absences, or loss of interest in schoolwork.
- **Physical Symptoms**: Complaints of headaches, stomach-aches, or other unexplained physical symptoms that may be linked to emotional distress.
- **Emotional Indicators**: Persistent sadness, irritability, or anxiety; frequent crying; or expressions of hopelessness.
- **Social Indicators**: Difficulty making or keeping friends,

bullying behaviour, or being a victim of bullying.

- **Attention and Concentration**: Difficulty focusing, easily distracted, or hyperactive behaviour.

2.3 Screening and Assessment Tools

Effective screening and assessment tools are essential for identifying mental health issues in students. These tools can help educators and mental health professionals determine the severity of symptoms and the need for further evaluation or intervention.

Strengths and Difficulties Questionnaire (SDQ)

The SDQ is a brief behavioural screening questionnaire that assesses 25 attributes, divided between five scales: emotional symptoms, conduct problems, hyperactivity/inattention, peer relationship problems, and prosocial behaviour (Goodman, 2001). It is widely used in schools for initial screening.

Patient Health Questionnaire-9 (PHQ-9)

The PHQ-9 is a self-administered scale for assessing depression. It includes nine items based on the criteria for diagnosing depressive disorders and is suitable for use with adolescents (Kroenke, Spitzer, & Williams, 2001).

Generalized Anxiety Disorder-7 (GAD-7)

The GAD-7 is a screening tool for identifying generalized anxiety disorder. It consists of seven items that measure the severity of anxiety symptoms (Spitzer, Kroenke, Williams, & Löwe, 2006).

Vanderbilt ADHD Diagnostic Rating Scale

This scale is used to assess symptoms of ADHD in children. It includes items that evaluate inattention, hyperactivity, impulsivity, and performance in academic and social settings.

Autism Diagnostic Observation Schedule (ADOS)

The ADOS is a standardized assessment tool for diagnosing autism spectrum disorders. It involves structured and semi-structured tasks that assess communication, social interaction, and play or imaginative use of materials.

2.4 The Role of Teachers and Staff in Identification

Teachers and school staff are on the front lines when it comes to observing and identifying potential mental health issues in students. Their regular interaction with students places them in an ideal position to notice changes in behaviour, mood, and academic performance.

Observational Skills

Teachers can use their observational skills to identify students who may be struggling with mental health issues. This includes paying attention to:

- Changes in attendance and punctuality
- Fluctuations in academic performance
- Behavioural changes in the classroom
- Interpersonal dynamics with peers

Creating an Open Environment

Creating an environment where students feel safe and supported to talk about their mental health is crucial. Teachers can:

- Foster a supportive classroom atmosphere
- Encourage open conversations about mental health
- Provide reassurance and validation to students expressing concerns

Training and Professional Development

Regular training and professional development can equip teachers with the skills needed to recognize and address mental health issues. This can include:

- Workshops on mental health awareness
- Training in specific screening tools and referral processes
- Strategies for managing classroom behaviour related to mental health issues

2.5 Case Studies: Early Identification and Intervention

Real-life case studies can provide valuable insights into the processes and outcomes of early identification and intervention in school settings.

Case Study 1: Addressing Anxiety Through Early Intervention

A middle school student exhibiting signs of anxiety, such as frequent absenteeism and difficulty concentrating, was identified by a teacher trained in the GAD-7 screening tool. Early intervention involved collaboration with the school counsellor, who provided cognitive-behavioural strategies and worked with the student's parents to create a supportive home environment. The student showed significant improvement in both academic performance and emotional well-being.

Case Study 2: Supporting a Student with Depression

A high school student displaying persistent sadness and a sudden decline in grades was referred to the school psychologist after a teacher observed these changes. Using the PHQ-9, the psychologist identified symptoms of depression and initiated a support plan that included regular counseling sessions and academic accommodations. The student gradually regained interest in school activities and improved academically.

Case Study 3: Managing ADHD in the Classroom

An elementary school teacher noticed a student with consistent inattentiveness and impulsive behaviour. After completing the Conners CBRS, the student was diagnosed with ADHD. The teacher, along with a special education coordinator, implemented individualized instructional strategies and behavioural interventions. The student's engagement and academic performance improved significantly over time.

Identifying mental health issues in students is a critical step in providing timely and effective support. By understanding common mental health disorders, recognizing the signs and symptoms, utilizing appropriate screening and assessment tools, and empowering teachers and staff, schools can create a proactive approach to mental health. Early identification and intervention can significantly improve students' academic performance and overall well-being, fostering a healthier and more supportive educational environment.

Chapter 3

Mental Health and Academic Performance

3.1 The Connection Between Mental Health and Learning

Mental health is intricately connected to academic performance. Numerous studies have established that mental health issues can significantly impede a student's ability to learn, concentrate, and perform academically. Understanding this connection is essential for educators, parents, and policymakers to create supportive environments that foster both mental well-being and academic success.

Cognitive Functioning

Mental health disorders such as anxiety and depression can severely impact cognitive functioning. Anxiety can lead to difficulties in concentration, memory, and processing information, which are critical for learning and academic performance. Similarly, depression is often associated with impaired cognitive abilities, including attention, decision-making, and problem-solving (Levine et al., 2007).

A study by Owens, Stevenson, Hadwin, and Norgate (2012) found that students with higher levels of anxiety performed worse on tasks requiring working memory and cognitive flexibility. These cognitive impairments can result in lower academic achievement and difficulties in meeting academic expectations.

Emotional and Behavioural Regulation

Mental health significantly influences a student's ability to regulate emotions and behaviour, which are crucial for success in the classroom. Students with mental health issues may struggle with emotional outbursts, impulsivity, and difficulty following classroom rules. These behaviours can disrupt their learning and that of their peers (Reinke, Herman, & Stormont, 2013).

Effective emotional and behavioural regulation is linked to better academic outcomes. For instance, students who can manage their emotions and behaviour are more likely to engage positively in the classroom, participate in learning activities, and develop healthy relationships with peers and teachers (Durlak et al., 2011).

Attendance and Engagement

Mental health problems can lead to increased absenteeism and decreased school engagement. Students suffering from conditions like anxiety, depression, or chronic stress may find it challenging to attend school regularly, resulting in frequent absences. Chronic absenteeism can disrupt learning continuity and lead to academic underachievement (Kearney & Graczyk, 2014).

Engagement in school activities is also affected by mental health. Students experiencing mental health issues may withdraw from school activities, show less interest in academic pursuits, and avoid social interactions. This disengagement can further exacerbate academic difficulties and hinder educational attainment (Fredricks, Blumenfeld, & Paris, 2004).

3.2 How Anxiety and Depression Affect Academic Achievement

Anxiety

Anxiety disorders are among the most common mental health issues affecting students, and their impact on academic achievement can be profound. Anxiety can manifest in various ways, including generalized anxiety disorder, social anxiety, and test anxiety, each affecting academic performance differently.

- **Generalized Anxiety Disorder (GAD)**: Students with GAD may experience pervasive worry that interferes with their ability to focus on schoolwork. This constant state of worry can lead to difficulties in completing assignments, taking exams, and participating in class discussions (Mazzone et al., 2007).

- **Social Anxiety**: Students with social anxiety may avoid participating in class or engaging in group activities, which are essential for collaborative learning. This avoidance can result in missed learning opportunities and lower academic performance (Woodward & Fergusson, 2001).

- **Test Anxiety**: Test anxiety can significantly impair a student's ability to perform well on exams. Students with test anxiety may experience physical symptoms like sweating and rapid heartbeat, cognitive impairments like difficulty concentrating, and emotional distress, all of which can negatively impact test performance (Zeidner, 1998).

Depression

Depression is another common mental health issue that can severely affect academic achievement. The symptoms of depression, such as persistent sadness, loss of interest in activities, and fatigue, can make it difficult for students to engage in schoolwork and maintain academic performance.

- **Motivation and Energy**: Depression often leads to decreased motivation and energy levels, making it challenging for students to complete assignments and study for exams. This lack of motivation can result in missed deadlines, incomplete work, and lower grades (Richardson, Abraham, & Bond, 2012).

- **Cognitive Impairments**: Depression can impair cognitive functions such as attention, memory, and executive functioning. These cognitive impairments can make it difficult for students to learn new information, retain knowledge, and apply critical thinking skills in their coursework (Eysenck et al., 2007).

- **Social Withdrawal**: Depressed students may withdraw from social interactions, including those that take place in the classroom. This withdrawal can lead to isolation, reduced participation in group work, and missed collaborative learning experiences (Kovacs & Goldston, 1991).

3.3 Strategies to Support Students with Mental Health Challenges

Schools and educators play a crucial role in supporting students with mental health challenges. Implementing effective strategies can help enhance academic performance and overall well-being. These strategies include creating a supportive environment, providing targeted interventions, and promoting overall well-being.

Creating a Supportive Environment

- **Positive School Climate**: Developing a positive school

climate where students feel safe, respected, and valued is crucial. This involves promoting inclusivity, preventing bullying, and encouraging positive relationships between students and staff (Thapa, Cohen, Guffey, & Higgins-D'Alessandro, 2013).

- **Mental Health Education**: Integrating mental health education into the curriculum can help students understand and manage their mental health. This education can reduce stigma and encourage students to seek help when needed (Wei, Kutcher, & Morgan, 2013).

-

Providing Targeted Interventions

- **Counselling Services**: Schools should provide access to school counsellors, psychologists, and social workers who can offer individual and group counselling. These professionals can help students develop coping strategies, address emotional and behavioural issues, and improve their overall well-being (Reback, 2010).
- **Academic Accommodations**: Providing academic accommodations, such as extended time for tests, flexible deadlines, and modified assignments, can help students with mental health challenges succeed academically. These accommodations can be tailored to meet the specific needs of each student (Madaus, 2008).

Promoting Overall Well-Being

- **Social and Emotional Learning (SEL)**: Implementing SEL programs can help students develop essential skills for managing emotions, building relationships, and making responsible decisions. These skills are critical for both mental health and academic success (Durlak et al., 2011).

- **Physical Health and Wellness**: Encouraging physical activity, healthy eating, and adequate sleep can positively impact students' mental health and academic performance. Schools can promote wellness through physical education classes, nutrition programs, and initiatives that encourage healthy lifestyle choices (Basch, 2011).

3.4 Promoting a Healthy Learning Environment

A healthy learning environment supports the mental health of all students and enhances their academic performance. Key components of a healthy learning environment include:

Teacher Training and Professional Development

Providing teachers with training on mental health awareness, classroom management, and supportive teaching strategies can equip them to better support students with mental health challenges. Ongoing professional development ensures that teachers stay informed about best practices and new research in the field of mental health and education (Jennings & Greenberg, 2009).

Parental Involvement

Engaging parents in their children's education and mental health can create a strong support network. Schools can offer workshops, resources, and communication channels to help parents understand mental health issues and support their children's academic and emotional needs (Berthelsen & Walker, 2008).

Collaboration with Community Resources

Schools can enhance their support systems by collaborating with community organizations and mental health professionals. Partnerships with local mental health clinics, non-profits, and health agencies can provide additional resources and services to support students' mental health (Weist et al., 2014).

3.5 Success Stories: Overcoming Mental Health Barriers to Academic Success

Success stories of students overcoming mental health barriers to achieve academic success highlight the importance of supportive interventions and the resilience of individuals facing these challenges. These narratives demonstrate how targeted strategies, supportive environments, and personal determination can lead to positive outcomes, providing inspiration and practical insights for educators, parents, and students alike.

Case Study 1: John's Journey with ADHD

Background

John, a high school student, was diagnosed with Attention-Deficit/Hyperactivity Disorder (ADHD) in middle school. His symptoms included difficulty concentrating, impulsive behaviour, and challenges in organizing tasks. These issues led to poor academic performance and frequent disciplinary actions.

Intervention

John's school implemented a multi-tiered system of supports (MTSS) tailored to his needs:

- **Academic Accommodations**: John received extended time on tests, breaks during long tasks, and a structured environment with clear, consistent expectations.

- **Behavioural Interventions**: The school counsellor worked with John on behavioural strategies, such as using a planner to organize tasks and breaking assignments into smaller, manageable parts.

- **Counselling and Support**: Regular meetings with the school psychologist provided John with coping strategies to manage his impulsivity and improve his focus.

Outcome

With these supports, John's academic performance improved significantly. His grades increased from Cs and Ds to As and Bs. Additionally, John's self-esteem and confidence grew as he experienced success in school. He graduated with honours and was accepted into a reputable college where he continues to thrive.

Case Study 2: Emma's Triumph Over Depression

Background

Emma, a high school junior, struggled with depression following her parents' divorce. She experienced persistent sadness, lack of motivation, and difficulty concentrating on her studies, leading to a noticeable decline in her academic performance.

Intervention

Emma's school adopted a holistic approach to support her mental health:

- **Counselling Services**: Emma began weekly sessions with the school counsellor to explore her feelings and develop coping strategies.
- **Peer Support Group**: She joined a peer support group facilitated by the school, providing a safe space to share experiences and gain support from others facing similar challenges.
- **Academic Adjustments**: Teachers offered flexibility with deadlines and additional tutoring sessions to help Emma catch up on missed work.

Outcome

With these interventions, Emma gradually regained her motivation and interest in school. Her grades improved, and she became more engaged in class activities. By her senior year, Emma was an active participant in the school's drama club and graduated with a strong academic record, gaining admission to her first-choice university.

Case Study 3: Sarah's Success with Anxiety Management

Background

Sarah, a middle school student, dealt with severe anxiety that affected her ability to participate in class and complete assignments. Her anxiety was particularly intense during exams, leading to panic attacks and poor test performance.

Intervention

The school implemented several strategies to help Sarah manage her anxiety:

- **Anxiety Reduction Techniques**: Sarah learned relaxation techniques, such as deep breathing and mindfulness, through sessions with the school counsellor.
- **Test Accommodations**: She was provided with a quiet room and extra time for taking exams, reducing her anxiety and allowing her to perform to her true potential.
- **Parental Involvement**: The school engaged Sarah's parents in her support plan, ensuring consistency in strategies used at home and school.

Outcome

With these supports, Sarah's anxiety decreased significantly. She began to participate more in class, and her test performance improved. By the end of the school year, Sarah's grades reflected her true capabilities, and she felt more confident in her ability to handle stressful situations. Her success continued into high school, where she became a student ambassador, helping others with similar challenges.

Case Study 4: Michael's Achievement Despite Social Anxiety

Background

Michael, a high school freshman, suffered from social anxiety, making it difficult for him to engage with peers and participate in group activities. His anxiety led to isolation and affected his academic performance, particularly in subjects requiring group work.

Intervention

Michael's school provided a comprehensive support plan:

- **Social Skills Training**: Michael participated in a social skills group led by the school psychologist, where he practiced interacting with peers in a structured and supportive setting.
- **Gradual Exposure**: Teachers gradually introduced Michael to group activities, starting with smaller, less intimidating groups and slowly increasing the group size as his confidence grew.
- **Encouragement and Positive Reinforcement**: Michael's efforts and progress were consistently acknowledged and praised by teachers and peers, reinforcing his self-esteem.

Outcome

Through these interventions, Michael's social anxiety reduced significantly. He began to participate more actively in group work and developed friendships that provided additional support. His academic performance improved as he felt more comfortable and engaged in the classroom. Michael went on to become a peer mentor, helping other students overcome social challenges.

Case Study 5: Leah's Recovery from Trauma

Background

Leah, a middle school student, experienced trauma following a car accident, leading to symptoms of Post-Traumatic Stress Disorder (PTSD). Her symptoms included flashbacks, nightmares, and difficulty concentrating, severely impacting her school performance.

Intervention

Leah's school adopted a trauma-informed approach to support her recovery:

- **Trauma-Focused Therapy**: Leah received trauma-focused cognitive-behavioural therapy (TF-CBT) from the school psychologist to address her PTSD symptoms.
- **Safe Spaces**: The school provided Leah with a quiet, safe space where she could go if she felt overwhelmed.
- **Teacher Training**: Leah's teachers received training on trauma-informed practices, enabling them to provide appropriate support and accommodations.

Outcome

With these supports, Leah's PTSD symptoms gradually decreased. She became more comfortable in the school environment and was able to concentrate better on her studies. Her academic performance improved, and she started participating in extracurricular activities again. Leah's resilience and the school's support enabled her to overcome significant challenges and succeed academically.

These success stories illustrate the transformative impact that targeted mental health interventions can have on students' academic performance and overall well-being. By creating supportive environments, providing tailored interventions, and fostering resilience, schools can help students overcome mental health barriers and achieve their full potential. These narratives serve as powerful reminders of the importance of mental health support in education and the positive outcomes that can result from comprehensive and compassionate approaches.

Chapter 4

Creating a Supportive School Environment

Creating a supportive school environment is essential for promoting mental health and well-being among students. A positive school climate not only enhances academic performance but also fosters emotional and social development. This chapter explores various strategies and practices that schools can implement to create a nurturing and supportive environment for all students.

4.1 Building a Culture of Wellbeing

A culture of well-being within a school setting involves creating an environment where mental health is prioritized, and every student feels valued and supported. This can be achieved through the following approaches:

Promoting Inclusivity and Diversity

Inclusivity and diversity are fundamental to a supportive school environment. Schools should celebrate diversity in all its forms, including cultural, racial, and socioeconomic differences. Promoting inclusivity involves:

- **Cultural Competence Training**: Providing training for staff and students to understand and appreciate cultural differences, which can reduce prejudice and promote a more inclusive school climate (Gay, 2010).
- **Inclusive Policies**: Implementing policies that protect all students from discrimination and ensure equal opportunities for participation in school activities.

Encouraging Student Voice and Participation

Allowing students to have a voice in school decisions and activities fosters a sense of ownership and belonging. This can be achieved by:

- **Student Councils and Committees**: Creating platforms where students can express their opinions and contribute to school governance.
- **Feedback Mechanisms**: Regularly soliciting feedback from students about their experiences and suggestions for improvement.

4.2 Anti-Bullying Programs and Their Impact

Bullying can have severe consequences for a student's mental health and academic performance. Implementing effective anti-bullying programs is crucial for creating a safe and supportive school environment.

Components of Effective Anti-Bullying Programs

- **Whole-School Approach**: Anti-bullying programs should involve the entire school community, including students, staff, and parents. A whole-school approach ensures that everyone is committed to creating a bully-free environment (Rigby, 2012).
- **Clear Policies and Procedures**: Establishing clear policies and procedures for reporting and responding to bullying incidents is essential. These policies should be communicated to all members of the school community.
- **Education and Awareness**: Providing education about the effects of bullying and promoting empathy and respect among students can help prevent bullying behaviours.

Evidence of Impact

Research has shown that comprehensive anti-bullying programs can significantly reduce the incidence of bullying in schools. For example, the Olweus Bullying Prevention Program has been widely studied and found to reduce bullying by 20-70% (Olweus & Limber, 2010). These programs not only decrease bullying incidents but also improve the overall school climate and student well-being.

4.3 Encouraging Open Conversations About Mental Health

Creating an environment where mental health can be openly discussed is crucial for reducing stigma and encouraging students to seek help when needed. Strategies to promote open conversations about mental health include:

Mental Health Education

Incorporating mental health education into the curriculum helps students understand mental health issues and recognize the importance of seeking help. Topics can include:

- **Understanding Mental Health**: Teaching students about different mental health conditions and their symptoms.
- **Coping Strategies**: Providing students with tools and techniques to manage stress and anxiety.

Peer Support Programs

Peer support programs involve training students to provide support to their peers, creating a network of help within the student body. Benefits of peer support programs include:

- **Increased Accessibility**: Students may feel more comfortable talking to peers about their mental health issues.
- **Empowerment**: Peer supporters gain valuable skills and experience, enhancing their own personal development.

4.4 The Importance of Social and Emotional Learning (SEL)

Social and Emotional Learning (SEL) is a critical component of a supportive school environment. SEL programs teach students essential skills for managing emotions, building relationships, and making responsible decisions.

Key Components of SEL Programs

- **Self-Awareness**: Helping students understand their own emotions, strengths, and areas for growth.
- **Self-Management**: Teaching strategies for regulating emotions and behaviors, such as mindfulness and stress management techniques.
- **Social Awareness**: Promoting empathy and understanding of others' perspectives.
- **Relationship Skills**: Developing communication and conflict resolution skills.
- **Responsible Decision-Making**: Encouraging thoughtful and ethical decision-making processes.
-

Evidence of Effectiveness

Research has demonstrated that SEL programs can have a positive impact on students' mental health and academic performance. A meta-analysis by Durlak et al. (2011) found that students who participated in SEL programs showed improved social and emotional skills, attitudes, and behaviour, as well as an 11% gain in academic achievement.

4.5 Best Practices from Schools Around the World

Schools across the globe have implemented innovative practices to create supportive environments that promote mental health and well-being. Some of these best practices include:

Finland: Holistic Approach to Education

Finland's education system is renowned for its holistic approach, which emphasizes the well-being of students alongside academic achievement. Key practices include:

- **Flexible Learning Environments**: Classrooms are designed to be flexible and comfortable, promoting a relaxed learning atmosphere.

- **Emphasis on Play and Physical Activity**: Regular breaks and physical activity are integrated into the school day, supporting physical and mental health.

Canada: Focus on Mental Health Literacy

Canada has made significant strides in integrating mental health literacy into the education system. Initiatives include:

- **The Mental Health Commission of Canada's School-Based Mental Health Programs**: These programs provide resources and training for teachers to incorporate mental health education into their classrooms (Kutcher & Wei, 2013).
- **Provincial Strategies**: Provinces like Ontario have developed comprehensive mental health strategies that include school-based interventions and supports.

Australia: Resilience Programs

Australian schools have implemented resilience programs aimed at building students' capacity to cope with stress and adversity. Examples include:

- **The Kids Matter Initiative**: A national mental health initiative that provides schools with a framework to support students' mental health and well-being (Slee et al., 2009).
- **Mind Matters**: A mental health initiative for secondary schools that promotes a whole-school approach to mental health (Wyn et al., 2000).

Creating a supportive school environment is essential for promoting mental health and academic success. By building a culture of well-being, implementing anti-bullying programs, encouraging open conversations about mental health, and integrating social and emotional learning, schools can foster an environment where all students can thrive. Learning from best practices around the world can provide valuable insights and inspiration for enhancing mental health support in schools. Through these efforts, schools can play a pivotal role in supporting the mental health and well-being of their students, preparing them for success both in and out of the classroom.

Chapter 5
The Role of Parents and Guardians

Parents and guardians play a crucial role in supporting the mental health and well-being of their children. Their involvement can significantly influence a child's emotional and academic development. This chapter explores various ways in which parents and guardians can contribute to their children's mental health, the importance of recognizing and addressing home-based stressors, effective communication strategies between parents and teachers, and the resources available to support families.

5.1 Engaging Parents in Mental Health Initiatives

Active parental involvement in mental health initiatives can create a robust support system for children, bridging the gap between home and school environments.

Importance of Parental Engagement

Research has consistently shown that parental involvement in a child's education is linked to better academic performance, improved behaviour, and enhanced emotional well-being (Epstein, 2011). When parents are engaged in mental health initiatives, they are better equipped to:

- **Recognize Signs of Mental Health Issues**: Parents who are educated about mental health can identify early warning signs and seek timely intervention.
- **Support at Home**: Engaged parents can create a supportive home environment that complements the mental health strategies implemented at school.
- **Advocate for Their Child**: Informed parents can advocate for appropriate resources and support services for their children.

Strategies for Engagement

Schools can adopt several strategies to encourage parental involvement in mental health initiatives:

- **Workshops and Training**: Offering workshops and training sessions on mental health topics can empower parents with knowledge and skills to support their children.
- **Regular Communication**: Maintaining open and consistent communication with parents through newsletters, meetings, and digital platforms can keep them informed about mental health programs and initiatives.
- **Parent-Teacher Associations (PTAs)**: Involving parents in PTAs can provide them with a platform to voice their concerns, share ideas, and participate in decision-making processes related to mental health.

5.2 Recognizing and Addressing Home-Based Stressors

Home-based stressors can significantly impact a child's mental health. Recognizing and addressing these stressors is essential for creating a stable and supportive environment for children.

Common Home-Based Stressors

- **Family Conflict**: Frequent arguments and conflicts within the family can create a stressful environment for children, affecting their emotional well-being.
- **Financial Stress**: Economic hardships can lead to anxiety and insecurity, impacting a child's mental health.
- **Parental Mental Health Issues**: Parents dealing with their own mental health problems may struggle to provide the necessary support and stability for their children.

Addressing Home-Based Stressors

- **Family Counselling**: Engaging in family counselling can help address underlying conflicts and improve family dynamics.
- **Financial Support Programs**: Accessing community resources and financial support programs can alleviate economic stress and provide stability.
- **Parental Mental Health Support**: Parents should be encouraged to seek help for their mental health issues to ensure they can support their children effectively.

5.3 Communication Strategies for Parents and Teachers

Effective communication between parents and teachers is vital for supporting a child's mental health and academic success. Building a strong partnership requires mutual trust, respect, and ongoing dialogue.

Establishing Open Lines of Communication

- **Regular Updates**: Teachers should provide regular updates on a child's progress, behaviour, and any concerns that may arise. This can be done through emails, phone calls, or parent-teacher conferences.
- **Two-Way Communication**: Encouraging parents to share their observations and concerns about their child can provide teachers with a comprehensive understanding of the child's needs.
- **Confidentiality and Sensitivity**: Maintaining confidentiality and handling sensitive information with care is crucial for building trust between parents and teachers.

Collaborative Problem-Solving

When issues arise, a collaborative approach to problem-solving can be beneficial. This involves:

- **Identifying the Problem**: Clearly defining the issue and its impact on the child's mental health and academic performance.
- **Developing a Plan**: Creating a joint action plan that includes specific strategies and interventions to address the problem.
- **Monitoring Progress**: Regularly reviewing the child's progress and making necessary adjustments to the plan.

5.4 Resources and Support Systems for Families

Access to resources and support systems can greatly assist families in managing mental health challenges and promoting well-being.

School-Based Resources

- **School Counsellors and Psychologists**: Many schools offer counselling and psychological services that can support students and their families.
- **Parent Workshops**: Schools can organize workshops on topics such as stress management, parenting skills, and mental health awareness.

Community Resources

- **Mental Health Services**: Local mental health clinics and organizations can provide counselling, therapy, and support groups for families.
- **Financial Assistance Programs**: Community organizations often offer financial assistance programs to help families cope with economic stressors.

Online Resources

- **Educational Websites**: Websites such as the National Alliance on Mental Illness (NAMI) and the American Psychological Association (APA) offer valuable information and resources for parents.
- **Support Groups**: Online support groups and forums can provide parents with a platform to share experiences and gain support from others facing similar challenges.

5.5 Real-Life Examples: Parental Involvement and Student Wellbeing

Real-life examples of parental involvement can provide valuable insights and inspiration for other families. Here are a few success stories:

Case Study 1: The Johnson Family

The Johnsons noticed their son, Alex, was struggling with anxiety and declining academic performance. They engaged with the school counsellor and attended workshops on anxiety management. By implementing consistent routines at home and maintaining regular communication with teachers, Alex's anxiety levels decreased, and his academic performance improved.

Case Study 2: The Ramirez Family

Maria Ramirez, a single mother, faced financial hardships that affected her children's well-being. She accessed community financial assistance programs and enrolled in a parent support group offered by the school. With the support she received, Maria was able to create a more stable home environment, and her children's emotional and academic outcomes improved.

Case Study 3: The Lee Family

The Lee family struggled with their daughter, Sophie's, social anxiety. They worked closely with her teachers to develop a plan that included social skills training and gradual exposure to social situations. The Lees also sought help from a child psychologist. Over time, Sophie became more comfortable in social settings, participated more in school activities, and her academic performance improved.

Parents and guardians play a vital role in supporting their children's mental health and academic success. By engaging in mental health initiatives, recognizing and addressing home-based stressors, maintaining effective communication with teachers, and utilizing available resources, families can create a supportive environment that fosters well-being and academic achievement. The collaborative efforts of parents, teachers, and the community are essential for promoting the mental health and overall success of students.

Chapter 6
Professional Development for Educators

Professional development for educators is crucial in fostering a school environment that supports the mental health and well-being of students. As frontline responders to student needs, teachers and school staff must be equipped with the knowledge and skills to identify, address, and support mental health issues. This chapter explores the importance of professional development, key training areas, effective professional development models, and real-life examples of successful programs.

6.1 Mental Health Training for Teachers
Importance of Mental Health Training

Teachers play a pivotal role in the early identification and support of students with mental health issues. However, many educators feel unprepared to address these challenges due to a lack of training. According to a survey by the American Federation of Teachers (AFT), 61% of teachers reported that they were not equipped to support students' mental health needs (AFT, 2017).

Mental health training for teachers can lead to:

- **Early Identification**: Teachers trained in mental health are better able to recognize early signs of mental health issues and refer students to appropriate support services.

- **Improved Student Outcomes**: Students receive timely and appropriate support, leading to better academic and emotional outcomes.

- **Teacher Well-being**: Educators equipped with mental health skills experience less stress and greater job satisfaction as they feel more competent in managing classroom challenges.

Key Training Areas

- **Recognizing Mental Health Issues**: Training should cover the signs and symptoms of common mental health disorders such as anxiety, depression, ADHD, and trauma-related conditions.

- **Intervention Strategies**: Educators should learn effective classroom strategies to support students with mental health issues, including de-escalation techniques and positive behaviour supports.

- **Referral Processes**: Teachers need to understand the school's referral processes for mental health services and how to collaborate with counsellors, psychologists, and social workers.

- **Self-Care for Educators**: Training should also emphasize the importance of self-care and provide strategies for teachers to manage their own stress and prevent burnout.

6.2 Identifying Burnout and Stress in Educators

Understanding Burnout

Burnout is a state of emotional, physical, and mental exhaustion caused by prolonged stress. It is particularly prevalent in the teaching profession due to high workloads, emotional demands, and limited resources. Symptoms of burnout include:

- **Emotional Exhaustion**: Feeling drained and overwhelmed.

- **Depersonalization**: Developing a cynical attitude towards students and colleagues.

- **Reduced Personal Accomplishment**: Feeling ineffective and unaccomplished in one's role (Maslach & Leiter, 2016).

Impact on Teachers and Students

Burnout can negatively affect teachers' mental health, leading to increased absenteeism, reduced teaching effectiveness, and a higher turnover rate. Additionally, teacher burnout can impact students, resulting in lower academic achievement and decreased engagement.

Strategies to Address Burnout

- **Professional Development**: Providing training on stress management, time management, and self-care can help reduce burnout.
- **Supportive School Culture**: Creating a supportive and collaborative school environment can help mitigate the effects of burnout.
- **Work-Life Balance**: Encouraging teachers to maintain a healthy work-life balance and providing resources such as mental health days and access to counselling services.

6.3 Self-Care Strategies for School Staff

Importance of Self-Care

Self-care is essential for educators to maintain their well-being and effectiveness. When teachers prioritize their own mental health, they are better equipped to support their students. Self-care strategies include:

- **Physical Health**: Encouraging regular exercise, healthy eating, and sufficient sleep.
- **Emotional Health**: Practicing mindfulness, meditation, and relaxation techniques.
- **Professional Support**: Participating in professional learning communities and seeking mentorship.

Practical Self-Care Strategies

- **Mindfulness and Relaxation**: Incorporating mindfulness practices such as deep breathing, meditation, and yoga into daily routines.
- **Professional Boundaries**: Setting clear boundaries between work and personal life to prevent burnout.
- **Peer Support**: Building a network of colleagues for mutual support and sharing of best practices.

6.4 Building Resilience in the Educational Workforce
Resilience Training

Resilience training helps educators develop the capacity to recover from setbacks, adapt to change, and keep going in the face of adversity. Key components of resilience training include:

- **Positive Thinking**: Encouraging a positive outlook and focusing on strengths.
- **Problem-Solving Skills**: Teaching effective problem-solving techniques to handle challenges.
- **Emotional Regulation**: Developing strategies to manage emotions and reduce stress.

Implementing Resilience Programs

- **Workshops and Seminars**: Offering regular workshops on resilience and stress management.
- **Mentorship Programs**: Pairing experienced teachers with new educators to provide guidance and support.
- **School-Wide Initiatives**: Creating a culture of resilience through school-wide initiatives and policies that promote well-being.

Benefits of Resilience Training

- **Improved Mental Health**: Teachers who are more resilient experience less stress and better mental health.
- **Enhanced Job Satisfaction**: Resilient educators report higher job satisfaction and a greater sense of accomplishment.
- **Positive School Climate**: A resilient workforce contributes to a positive school climate, benefiting both staff and students.

6.5 Case Studies: Successful Professional Development Programs

Case Study 1: The MindUP Program

The MindUP program, implemented in various schools across North America, focuses on mindfulness and social-emotional learning. Teachers receive training on integrating mindfulness practices into the classroom, which has led to:

- **Reduced Teacher Stress**: Educators report lower stress levels and greater emotional well-being.
- **Improved Student Behaviour**: Students demonstrate better self-regulation and reduced behavioural issues.

Case Study 2: The Teacher Resilience Project

The Teacher Resilience Project, conducted in Australian schools, provides comprehensive resilience training for educators. The program includes workshops on stress management, peer support groups, and ongoing mentorship. Outcomes include:

- **Increased Teacher Retention**: Schools participating in the project report higher teacher retention rates.
- **Enhanced Teaching Effectiveness**: Teachers feel more confident and effective in their roles.

Case Study 3: The Collaborative for Academic, Social, and Emotional Learning (CASEL)

CASEL's professional development programs focus on integrating social-emotional learning into the school curriculum. Training includes SEL curriculum development, classroom management techniques, and self-care for teachers. Benefits observed include:

- **Positive School Climate**: Schools with SEL integration report a more positive and supportive school climate.
- **Academic Gains**: Students in SEL-focused schools show improved academic performance and reduced emotional distress.

Professional development for educators is essential for creating a supportive school environment that promotes mental health and well-being. By providing training in mental health awareness, stress management, and resilience, schools can equip teachers with the skills they need to support their students effectively and maintain their own well-being. Successful professional development programs, such as MindUP and the Teacher Resilience Project, demonstrate the positive impact of investing in educators' professional growth and mental health. As schools continue to prioritize professional development, they will create healthier, more supportive environments for both teachers and students.

Chapter 7

Implementing School-Based Mental Health Programs

Implementing school-based mental health programs is crucial for addressing the mental health needs of students. Effective programs can enhance students' well-being, improve academic performance, and create a supportive school environment. This chapter explores the key components of successful school-based mental health programs, strategies for collaboration with mental health professionals, funding and sustainability considerations, methods for monitoring and evaluating program impact, and examples of successful programs.

7.1 Planning and Designing Effective Programs

Needs Assessment

The first step in implementing a school-based mental health program is conducting a thorough needs assessment. This involves gathering data to understand the specific mental health needs of the student population and identifying existing resources and gaps.

- **Surveys and Questionnaires**: Distributing surveys to students, parents, and staff to gather information on mental health concerns and priorities.
- **Focus Groups**: Conducting focus groups with students, parents, teachers, and community members to gain qualitative insights.
- **Data Analysis**: Reviewing existing data on attendance, academic performance, and behavioural incidents to identify trends and areas of concern (Levitt, Saka, Romanelli, & Hoagwood, 2007).

Program Design

Based on the needs assessment, schools can design tailored mental health programs that address the specific needs of their students. Key considerations in program design include:

- **Evidence-Based Practices**: Incorporating interventions and strategies that are supported by research and proven to be effective.
- **Comprehensive Approach**: Designing programs that address prevention, early intervention, and intensive support.
- **Student and Family Involvement**: Engaging students and families in the program design process to ensure their needs and preferences are considered (Kutcher & Wei, 2013).

7.2 Collaboration with Mental Health Professionals
Building Partnerships

Collaboration with mental health professionals is essential for the successful implementation of school-based programs. Schools can build partnerships with:

- **Local Mental Health Agencies**: Collaborating with local mental health clinics and agencies to provide additional resources and services.
- **University Partnerships**: Partnering with universities to access expertise, training, and research opportunities.
- **Community Organizations**: Engaging community organizations that specialize in mental health, such as non-profits and advocacy groups (Weist, Lever, Bradshaw, & Owens, 2014).

Integrated Services

Integrating mental health services within the school setting can improve accessibility and coordination of care. Strategies for integration include:

- **On-Site Mental Health Professionals**: Employing school counsellors, psychologists, and social workers who are available on-site to provide support and interventions.
- **Telehealth Services**: Utilizing telehealth platforms to offer remote counselling and mental health services, particularly in underserved areas.
- **Co-Located Services**: Partnering with external mental health providers to offer services on school premises (Hoover, Lever, Sachdev, & Brindis, 2017).

7.3 Funding and Sustainability of Mental Health Initiatives
Identifying Funding Sources

Sustainable funding is critical for the long-term success of school-based mental health programs. Potential funding sources include:

- **Federal and State Grants**: Applying for grants from government agencies that support mental health initiatives in schools.
- **Private Foundations**: Seeking funding from private foundations and philanthropic organizations that focus on education and mental health.
- **Community Fundraising**: Organizing community fundraising events and campaigns to generate support and resources.
- **School Budgets**: Allocating a portion of the school budget to support mental health programs and services (Adelman &

Taylor, 2006).

Budget Planning

Effective budget planning ensures that resources are allocated efficiently and sustainably. Key components of budget planning include:

- **Cost Analysis**: Identifying the costs associated with implementing and maintaining the program, including personnel, training, materials, and facilities.
- **Resource Allocation**: Allocating resources based on priorities identified in the needs assessment.
- **Financial Oversight**: Establishing financial oversight mechanisms to monitor spending and ensure accountability (Hoagwood, Olin, Kerker, Kratochwill, Crowe, & Saka, 2007).

7.4 Monitoring and Evaluating Program Impact Evaluation Framework

Monitoring and evaluating the impact of school-based mental health programs is essential for continuous improvement and accountability. An effective evaluation framework includes:

- **Baseline Data**: Collecting baseline data before program implementation to measure progress and impact.
- **Outcome Measures**: Identifying key outcome measures, such as changes in student mental health, academic performance, and behaviour.
- **Process Evaluation**: Assessing the implementation process to identify strengths and areas for improvement.
- **Feedback Mechanisms**: Establishing mechanisms for collecting feedback from students, parents, and staff (Mellin, Taylor, & Weist, 2011).

Data Collection and Analysis

Collecting and analysing data is crucial for evaluating program impact. Methods for data collection include:

- **Surveys and Questionnaires**: Administering surveys to gather quantitative and qualitative data on program outcomes.

- **Focus Groups and Interviews**: Conducting focus groups and interviews with stakeholders to gain in-depth insights.

- **Administrative Data**: Analysing administrative data, such as attendance records, disciplinary incidents, and academic performance (O'Donnell, Hawkins, & McCormick, 2008).

7.5 Examples of Successful School-Based Mental Health Programs

The Comprehensive School-Based Mental Health Program (CSBMHP)

The CSBMHP, implemented in several schools across the United States, focuses on providing comprehensive mental health services, including prevention, early intervention, and treatment. Key components of the program include:

- **Universal Prevention**: Implementing school-wide initiatives, such as social-emotional learning (SEL) programs, to promote mental health and prevent issues.

- **Targeted Interventions**: Providing targeted interventions for at-risk students, such as small group counselling and skill-building workshops.

- **Intensive Support**: Offering intensive support for students with significant mental health needs, including individual therapy and case management (Weist et al., 2014).

The Positive Behavioural Interventions and Supports (PBIS) Framework

PBIS is an evidence-based framework that aims to improve student behaviour and create a positive school climate. The PBIS framework includes:

- **Tier 1: Universal Interventions**: Implementing school-wide behavioural expectations and support for all students.
- **Tier 2: Targeted Interventions**: Providing additional support for students at risk of behavioural issues, such as small group interventions.
- **Tier 3: Intensive Interventions**: Offering individualized support for students with significant behavioural and mental health needs (Sugai & Horner, 2002).

The Healthy Environments and Response to Trauma in Schools (HEARTS) Program

The HEARTS program, developed by the University of California, San Francisco, focuses on creating trauma-informed schools that support students affected by trauma. Key components of the program include:

- **Trauma-Informed Training**: Providing training for educators and staff on understanding and responding to trauma.
- **Supportive Practices**: Implementing practices that promote safety, trustworthiness, and empowerment for students.
- **Collaboration**: Collaborating with mental health professionals to provide comprehensive support for students and families (Dorado, Martinez, McArthur, & Leibovitz, 2016).

Implementing school-based mental health programs is essential for addressing the mental health needs of students and creating a supportive school environment. By conducting thorough needs assessments, designing tailored programs, collaborating with mental health professionals, securing sustainable funding, and continuously monitoring and evaluating program impact, schools can effectively support the mental health and well-being of their students. Successful programs, such as CSBMHP, PBIS, and HEARTS, provide valuable examples of how comprehensive and integrated approaches can lead to positive outcomes for students and school communities.

Chapter 8

Crisis Management and Intervention

Effective crisis management and intervention are essential components of a comprehensive school mental health program. Schools must be prepared to handle a variety of crises, from natural disasters to mental health emergencies, to ensure the safety and well-being of students and staff. This chapter explores the development of crisis response plans, strategies for handling mental health emergencies, post-crisis support and recovery, collaboration with community resources, and lessons learned from past crises.

8.1 Developing Crisis Response Plans

Importance of a Crisis Response Plan

A well-developed crisis response plan provides a structured approach for managing emergencies, ensuring that all school personnel are prepared to act swiftly and effectively. Key components of a crisis response plan include:

- **Clear Communication Protocols**: Establishing clear lines of communication for notifying staff, students, parents, and emergency services.
- **Defined Roles and Responsibilities**: Assigning specific roles and responsibilities to school personnel to ensure a coordinated response.
- **Emergency Procedures**: Outlining procedures for various types of crises, including lockdowns, evacuations, and shelter-in-place protocols (Brock, Nickerson, Reeves, Jimerson, Lieberman, & Feinberg, 2009).

Steps to Develop a Crisis Response Plan

1. **Form a Crisis Response Team**: Assemble a team of school administrators, counsellors, nurses, teachers, and local

emergency responders.

2. **Conduct a Risk Assessment**: Identify potential risks and vulnerabilities within the school and community.
3. **Develop Protocols and Procedures**: Create detailed procedures for responding to different types of crises, including natural disasters, violence, and mental health emergencies.
4. **Train Staff and Students**: Provide regular training and drills to ensure that everyone knows their roles and responsibilities during a crisis.
5. **Review and Revise**: Continuously review and update the crisis response plan to address new threats and incorporate lessons learned from drills and actual incidents (Heath, Ryan, Dean, & Bingham, 2007).

8.2 Handling Mental Health Emergencies in Schools
Recognizing Mental Health Emergencies

Mental health emergencies can arise suddenly and may include situations such as suicidal ideation, severe panic attacks, or psychotic episodes. Recognizing the signs of a mental health emergency is crucial for prompt intervention. Signs may include:

- **Expressing Suicidal Thoughts**: Verbalizing a desire to harm oneself or making suicidal threats.
- **Severe Anxiety or Panic Attacks**: Displaying extreme fear or panic that interferes with daily activities.
- **Psychosis**: Exhibiting symptoms such as hallucinations, delusions, or disorganized thinking (NAMI, 2021).

Immediate Response Strategies

- **Stay Calm and Assess the Situation**: Remain calm and assess the severity of the situation to determine the appropriate response.

- **Ensure Safety**: Ensure the safety of the student and others. Remove any potential hazards and provide a safe environment.
- **Engage Support Services**: Contact school counsellors, psychologists, or local mental health crisis teams for immediate support.
- **Communicate with Parents and Guardians**: Inform parents or guardians about the situation and involve them in the intervention process (Brock et al., 2009).

Crisis Intervention Techniques

- **De-Escalation Techniques**: Use calming strategies and active listening to de-escalate the situation. Speak in a calm, reassuring tone and avoid confrontational language.
- **Suicide Prevention**: Implement protocols for assessing suicide risk and ensuring the student's safety. This may include constant supervision and referral to mental health professionals.
- **Referral to Professional Services**: Ensure that the student receives a thorough evaluation and appropriate follow-up care from mental health professionals (SAMHSA, 2019).

8.3 Post-Crisis Support and Recovery

Immediate Post-Crisis Support

After a crisis, providing immediate support is essential for helping students and staff recover. Strategies include:

- **Critical Incident Stress Debriefing (CISD)**: Conduct debriefing sessions for students and staff to discuss their experiences and emotions. These sessions can help normalize reactions and provide coping strategies.
- **Counselling Services**: Offer individual and group counselling to those affected by the crisis. Ensure that mental health professionals are available to provide ongoing support (Mitchell, 1983).

Long-Term Recovery

Long-term recovery efforts focus on restoring a sense of normalcy and addressing the ongoing mental health needs of the school community. Key components include:

- **Monitoring and Follow-Up**: Continuously monitor the mental health of students and staff and provide follow-up support as needed.
- **Reintegration Plans**: Develop plans to support students and staff as they reintegrate into the school environment. This may include academic accommodations and modified schedules.
- **Community Support**: Engage community resources and organizations to provide additional support and services during the recovery process (NCTSN, 2006).

8.4 Collaborating with Community Resources
Building Partnerships

Collaboration with community resources is vital for effective crisis management and recovery. Schools can build partnerships with:

- **Local Mental Health Agencies**: Partner with local mental health agencies to provide crisis intervention and ongoing support services.
- **Emergency Responders**: Establish relationships with local police, fire departments, and emergency medical services to ensure coordinated responses to crises.
- **Community Organizations**: Engage community organizations that specialize in crisis response, trauma recovery, and mental health support (Weist, Rubin, Moore, Adelsheim, & Wrobel, 2007).

Utilizing Community Resources

- **Crisis Hotlines**: Provide information about crisis hotlines and other emergency resources that students and staff can access.

- **Support Groups**: Connect students and families with local support groups that can provide peer support and resources.
- **Training and Workshops**: Offer training and workshops conducted by community experts on topics such as crisis intervention, trauma-informed care, and mental health first aid (SAMHSA, 2019).

8.5 Lessons Learned from Past Crises

Case Study 1: Sandy Hook Elementary School Shooting

The tragic shooting at Sandy Hook Elementary School in 2012 highlighted the importance of preparedness and response planning. Key lessons learned include:

- **Importance of Preparedness**: Comprehensive crisis response plans and regular drills are essential for ensuring a swift and coordinated response.
- **Mental Health Support**: Providing immediate and long-term mental health support for survivors is critical for recovery.
- **Community Collaboration**: Strong collaboration with community resources and mental health professionals can enhance the effectiveness of crisis response and recovery efforts (Cowan, Vaillancourt, Rossen, & Pollitt, 2013).

Case Study 2: Hurricane Katrina

The aftermath of Hurricane Katrina in 2005 demonstrated the need for effective crisis management and recovery strategies in the face of natural disasters. Key lessons learned include:

- **Flexibility and Adaptability**: Crisis response plans must be flexible and adaptable to address the unique challenges of different crises.
- **Support for Displaced Students**: Providing support for

displaced students, including academic accommodations and mental health services, is essential for their recovery.

- **Long-Term Recovery**: Long-term recovery efforts must focus on rebuilding communities and addressing the ongoing mental health needs of affected individuals (Kronenberg et al., 2010).

Effective crisis management and intervention are essential for ensuring the safety and well-being of students and staff. By developing comprehensive crisis response plans, handling mental health emergencies with care, providing post-crisis support, collaborating with community resources, and learning from past crises, schools can create a resilient and supportive environment. These efforts not only help schools respond effectively to crises but also promote the long-term mental health and well-being of the entire school community.

Chapter 9

Leveraging Technology for Mental Health Support

In an increasingly digital world, technology offers innovative solutions to support mental health in educational settings. From telehealth services to mental health apps, technology can enhance access to mental health resources, provide flexible support options, and foster a culture of well-being. This chapter explores various technological tools and strategies that schools can leverage to support the mental health of students and staff, the benefits and challenges of using technology, and examples of successful implementations.

9.1 Digital Tools and Apps for Mental Health

Types of Mental Health Apps

A variety of mental health apps are available to support students' well-being. These apps can offer self-help tools, mindfulness exercises, and crisis intervention resources. Common types of mental health apps include:

- **Mindfulness and Meditation Apps**: Apps like Headspace and Calm provide guided meditation and relaxation exercises to help manage stress and anxiety.
- **Mood Tracking Apps**: Apps such as Moodpath and Daylio allow users to track their moods and identify patterns that may indicate mental health issues.
- **Crisis Support Apps**: Apps like notOK and MY3 offer immediate support and resources for individuals experiencing a mental health crisis (Luxton, McCann, Bush, Mishkind, & Reger, 2011).

Integrating Apps into School Programs

Schools can integrate mental health apps into their programs by:

- **Recommending Apps**: Providing a list of vetted apps to students and parents as part of mental health education and support initiatives.
- **Incorporating Apps into Curriculum**: Using apps as tools in social-emotional learning (SEL) programs and wellness activities.
- **Training Students**: Offering workshops or guidance sessions on how to use mental health apps effectively and safely (Kumar, 2015).

9.2 Telehealth Services in Schools
The Rise of Telehealth

Telehealth has emerged as a crucial tool for delivering mental health services, especially in areas with limited access to traditional in-person counselling. Telehealth services can include video conferencing, phone calls, and online chat platforms, allowing students to connect with mental health professionals remotely.

- **Accessibility**: Telehealth can reach students in rural or underserved areas who may not have access to in-person mental health services.
- **Convenience**: Students can receive counselling from the comfort of their homes or schools, reducing barriers such as transportation and scheduling conflicts.
- **Anonymity**: Online platforms can provide a level of anonymity that may encourage students to seek help without fear of stigma (Yellowlees, Shore, & Roberts, 2010).

Implementing Telehealth in Schools

Schools can implement telehealth services by partnering with local mental health providers or utilizing telehealth platforms specifically designed for educational settings. Key steps include:

- **Selecting a Platform**: Choosing a secure, user-friendly telehealth platform that complies with privacy regulations such as HIPAA.
- **Training Staff**: Providing training for school counsellors and staff on how to use telehealth tools effectively.
- **Promoting Services**: Informing students and parents about the availability of telehealth services and how to access them (American Psychological Association, 2013).

9.3 Online Counselling and Support Groups
The Benefits of Online Counselling

Online counselling, also known as e-counselling or teletherapy, has gained popularity as an effective means of providing mental health support. It offers numerous advantages over traditional face-to-face counselling:

- **Accessibility**: Online counselling breaks down geographical barriers, making it easier for students in remote or underserved areas to access mental health services.
- **Convenience**: Sessions can be scheduled at flexible times, reducing the need for travel and allowing students to seek help from the comfort of their homes.
- **Anonymity**: The perceived anonymity of online counselling can make it easier for students to open up about their issues, especially those who are hesitant to seek face-to-face help (Barak, Hen, Boniel-Nissim, & Shapira, 2008).

Implementing Online Counselling in Schools

Schools can implement online counselling by partnering with licensed mental health professionals and using secure, HIPAA-compliant platforms. Steps to integrate online counselling include:

- **Selecting the Right Platform**: Choose a platform that ensures privacy and security, such as BetterHelp, Talkspace, or school-specific solutions like Kooth.
- **Training Staff**: Provide training for school counsellors on how to effectively conduct online sessions and maintain confidentiality.
- **Promoting the Service**: Inform students and parents about the availability of online counselling through newsletters, school websites, and social media (Harris, 2020).

The Role of Online Support Groups

Online support groups provide a platform for students to connect with peers facing similar challenges. These groups offer emotional support, reduce feelings of isolation, and foster a sense of community.

- **Peer Support**: Students can share experiences and coping strategies, providing mutual support and encouragement.
- **Moderation**: Trained professionals or counsellors should moderate online support groups to ensure a safe and supportive environment.
- **Resources and Education**: Support groups can provide valuable resources and information about mental health issues and coping mechanisms (Griffiths, Calear, Banfield, & Tam, 2009).

9.4 The Role of Social Media in Mental Health Awareness

Raising Awareness

Social media platforms like Instagram, Twitter, Facebook, and TikTok play a significant role in raising awareness about mental health. They provide a space for sharing information, resources, and personal stories, helping to reduce stigma and promote mental health literacy.

- **Campaigns and Hashtags**: Campaigns like #MentalHealthMatters and #EndTheStigma mobilize users to share their experiences and spread awareness.
- **Influencers and Advocates**: Mental health influencers and advocates use their platforms to educate followers and promote positive mental health practices (Naslund, Aschbrenner, Marsch, & Bartels, 2016).

Benefits and Challenges

While social media has numerous benefits for mental health awareness, it also presents challenges:

- **Benefits**:
  - **Increased Reach**: Social media can reach a large audience quickly and effectively.
  - **Community Building**: Users can find support and community through mental health groups and pages.
  - **Resource Sharing**: Easy access to mental health resources, articles, and helplines.
- **Challenges**:
  - **Misinformation**: The spread of inaccurate or harmful information about mental health.
  - **Cyberbullying**: Exposure to negative interactions and cyberbullying can exacerbate mental health issues.
  - **Comparison and Self-Esteem**: Constant comparison with others can negatively impact self-esteem and mental health (Valkenburg, Peter, & Schouten, 2006).

Guidelines for Safe Social Media Use

To maximize the benefits and mitigate the risks of social media use, schools can educate students on safe practices:

- **Critical Thinking**: Encourage critical evaluation of the information encountered online.
- **Digital Literacy**: Teach students about privacy settings and how to protect their personal information.
- **Balance and Moderation**: Promote a healthy balance between online and offline activities to prevent overuse and addiction (Livingstone, 2014).

9.5 Future Trends in Technology and Mental Health
Artificial Intelligence and Chatbots

Artificial Intelligence (AI) and chatbots are emerging as innovative tools for mental health support. These technologies can provide immediate, accessible support and resources:

- **AI-Powered Chatbots**: Chatbots like Woebot and Wysa offer cognitive-behavioral therapy (CBT) techniques, mindfulness exercises, and mood tracking.
- **24/7 Support**: Chatbots can provide support around the clock, offering immediate assistance and resources during crises (Fitzpatrick, Darcy, & Vierhile, 2017).

Virtual Reality Therapy

Virtual Reality (VR) therapy is an emerging trend that provides immersive experiences to treat mental health issues:

- **Exposure Therapy**: VR can be used for exposure therapy, helping students confront and manage their fears in a controlled environment.
- **Stress Reduction**: VR environments designed for relaxation and stress reduction can provide immersive mindfulness and meditation experiences (Maples-Keller, Bunnell, Kim, & Rothbaum, 2017).

Data Analytics and Personalization

Data analytics can be used to personalize mental health interventions and improve outcomes:

- **Predictive Analytics**: Analysing data to predict which students may be at risk for mental health issues and intervening early.
- **Personalized Interventions**: Using data to tailor interventions to individual needs, preferences, and progress (Topol, 2019).

Gamification and Mental Health

Gamification applies game design elements to non-game contexts to engage users and promote mental health:

- **Mental Health Apps**: Apps that incorporate gamification elements, such as rewards and challenges, to motivate users to complete mental health exercises and track their progress.
- **Educational Games**: Games designed to teach mental health concepts and coping strategies in an interactive and engaging

way (Johnson et al., 2016).

Technology offers a wide range of tools and platforms to support mental health in educational settings. By leveraging telehealth services, mental health apps, online counselling, support groups, and social media, schools can enhance access to mental health resources and support. As technology continues to evolve, emerging trends such as AI, VR therapy, data analytics, and gamification hold promise for further improving mental health outcomes. By staying informed and adopting innovative solutions, schools can create a supportive and inclusive environment that promotes the mental health and well-being of all students.

Chapter 10

Policy and Advocacy for Mental Health in Education

Effective policy and strong advocacy are essential for ensuring that mental health support in educational settings is prioritized and adequately funded. This chapter explores the current policies impacting mental health in education, the importance of advocacy efforts, strategies for advocating for change, international perspectives, and future challenges and opportunities.

10.1 Current Policies and Their Impact

Overview of Existing Policies

Policies at the federal, state, and local levels play a crucial role in shaping mental health services in schools. Key policies include:

- **Individuals with Disabilities Education Act (IDEA)**: Ensures students with disabilities, including mental health conditions, receive appropriate educational services and supports (U.S. Department of Education, 2004).

- **Every Student Succeeds Act (ESSA)**: Encourages schools to implement comprehensive mental health services and supports as part of a well-rounded education (U.S. Department of Education, 2015).

- **Mental Health in Schools Act**: Proposes increased funding for school-based mental health services, although its passage varies by legislative session (National Alliance on Mental Illness, 2021).

Impact of These Policies

- **Increased Access to Services**: Policies like IDEA and ESSA have led to increased access to mental health services for students, particularly those with identified needs.

- **Enhanced Funding**: These policies have resulted in more funding for school-based mental health programs, allowing schools to hire counsellors, psychologists, and social workers.
- **Standardization and Accountability**: Policies provide frameworks for standardizing mental health support and holding schools accountable for implementing necessary services (Center for Health and Health Care in Schools, 2016).

10.2 Advocacy Efforts and Their Importance

Why Advocacy Matters

Advocacy is essential for driving policy changes that improve mental health services in schools. Effective advocacy can lead to:

- **Increased Funding**: Advocacy efforts can secure additional funding for mental health programs.
- **Policy Changes**: Advocates can influence policymakers to pass laws that support mental health initiatives.
- **Raising Awareness**: Advocacy raises public awareness about the importance of mental health in education, reducing stigma and encouraging support (National Association of School Psychologists, 2017).

Key Advocacy Efforts

- **Grassroots Movements**: Local communities organizing to advocate for better mental health services in schools.
- **Professional Organizations**: Groups like the American School Counsellor Association (ASCA) and the National Association of School Psychologists (NASP) advocating for

policy changes at the national level.

- **Student and Parent Advocacy**: Students and parents speaking out about their experiences and the need for better mental health support in schools (Mental Health America, 2020).

10.3 How to Advocate for Change in Your Community

Advocacy is a powerful tool for driving change and improving mental health support in educational settings. By mobilizing community members, engaging with policymakers, and raising awareness, advocates can make a significant impact on the mental health landscape. This section provides a step-by-step guide to effective advocacy.

Steps to Effective Advocacy

1. **Educate Yourself**
   - **Understand Current Policies**: Familiarize yourself with existing mental health policies at the local, state, and federal levels. Resources like the U.S. Department of Education and local education departments provide valuable information.
   - **Identify Needs and Gaps**: Conduct a needs assessment to identify gaps in mental health services within your community. Use surveys, focus groups, and public data to gather insights.

2. **Build a Coalition**
   - **Partner with Stakeholders**: Collaborate with parents, students, teachers, mental health professionals, and community organizations. Building a diverse coalition can amplify your advocacy efforts.

- **Form Alliances**: Align with local mental health organizations and advocacy groups. Their expertise and resources can strengthen your campaign.

3. **Develop a Clear Message**
    - **Articulate Goals**: Clearly define the changes you want to see. Whether it's increasing funding for school counselors or implementing mental health education, your goals should be specific and achievable.
    - **Craft Your Message**: Develop a compelling message that highlights the importance of mental health support in schools. Use statistics, personal stories, and evidence-based arguments to make your case.

1. **Engage with Policymakers**
   - **Schedule Meetings**: Arrange meetings with local and state policymakers to discuss your concerns and proposed solutions. Be prepared with facts and persuasive arguments.
   - **Write Letters and Emails**: Send letters and emails to legislators expressing your support for mental health initiatives. Encourage others in your community to do the same.
   - **Use Social Media**: Leverage social media platforms to engage with policymakers and raise awareness. Tagging officials in your posts can increase visibility.
2. **Raise Public Awareness**
   - **Organize Events**: Host community events, such as town halls, workshops, and informational sessions, to educate the public about the importance of mental health in education.
   - **Media Outreach**: Reach out to local media outlets to cover your advocacy efforts. Write op-eds, participate in interviews, and use press releases to gain media attention.
   - **Petitions**: Create and circulate petitions to demonstrate community support for your cause. Present the signed petitions to policymakers as evidence of public backing.

Tools and Resources

- **Advocacy Toolkits**: Utilize toolkits from organizations like Mental Health America and the National Alliance on Mental

Illness (NAMI) that provide templates, talking points, and strategies for effective advocacy.

- **Training Programs**: Participate in training programs offered by advocacy groups to develop skills in lobbying, public speaking, and campaign management.
- **Online Platforms**: Use online platforms like Change.org for petitions and social media to organize and mobilize supporters (Advocates for Youth, 2020).

10.4 International Perspectives on Mental Health Policies
Comparative Analysis of Global Policies

Understanding how different countries approach mental health in education can provide valuable insights and best practices.

United Kingdom

- **Whole-School Approach**: The UK's policy emphasizes a whole-school approach to mental health, integrating mental health education and dedicated mental health leads in schools.
- **Government Support**: The UK government provides significant funding and resources for mental health programs in schools, including mandatory mental health education (Department for Education, 2018).

Australia

- **Programs like KidsMatter and MindMatters**: These frameworks focus on promoting mental health and well-being in schools through comprehensive support systems and government funding.
- **Collaborative Efforts**: Australian policies encourage

collaboration between schools, families, and community health services (Wyn et al., 2000).

Canada

- **School-Based Mental Health and Substance Abuse Consortium (SBMHSA):** This consortium works to integrate mental health services into schools, supported by provincial policies and funding.
- **National Guidelines:** Canada has developed national guidelines to ensure consistent mental health support across provinces (Kutcher & Wei, 2013).

Lessons Learned

- **Holistic Approaches**: Successful programs often take a holistic approach, integrating mental health education, support services, and community involvement.
- **Government Support**: Strong government backing and funding are crucial for the sustainability and effectiveness of school-based mental health programs.
- **Community and School Collaboration**: Effective policies often involve collaboration between schools, mental health professionals, and the community (OECD, 2015).

10.5 The Future of Mental Health in Education: Challenges and Opportunities

As the importance of mental health in education continues to gain recognition, several challenges and opportunities lie ahead. This section explores the emerging challenges schools may face and the potential opportunities for advancing mental health support in educational settings.

Emerging Challenges
Resource Limitations
Despite growing awareness and advocacy, many schools still face significant resource limitations. These constraints can hinder the implementation of comprehensive mental health programs.

- **Funding Shortfalls**: Limited budgets can restrict the hiring of qualified mental health professionals and the development of effective programs.
- **Staffing Challenges**: A shortage of trained mental health staff, such as counsellors and psychologists, can impede the delivery of services.
- **Infrastructure Needs**: Schools may lack the necessary infrastructure, such as private counselling spaces and technological tools, to support mental health initiatives (American Academy of Pediatrics, 2019).

Stigma and Awareness

Although progress has been made in reducing stigma, it remains a significant barrier to accessing mental health services.

- **Cultural Barriers**: Cultural perceptions and misunderstandings about mental health can prevent students and families from seeking help.
- **Awareness Gaps**: A lack of awareness about mental health issues and available resources can lead to underutilization of services.
- **Fear of Judgment**: Students may fear being judged or labelled by peers and educators if they disclose mental health struggles (Corrigan, Druss, & Perlick, 2014).

Policy Gaps

Inconsistent policies across regions can lead to disparities in the availability and quality of mental health services in schools.

- **Variable Implementation**: Differences in policy implementation at the state and local levels can result in unequal access to mental health support.
- **Lack of Standardization**: Inconsistent standards and guidelines for school-based mental health services can lead to variations in service quality.
- **Policy Enforcement**: Ensuring compliance with mental health policies can be challenging without adequate monitoring and accountability mechanisms (National Alliance on Mental Illness, 2021).

Opportunities for Advancement
Technological Innovations

Technological advancements offer promising opportunities to enhance mental health support in schools.

- **Telehealth Services**: Expanding telehealth services can improve access to mental health care, especially in underserved areas.
- **Mental Health Apps**: The development of mental health apps can provide students with accessible tools for managing their mental health.
- **Data Analytics**: Utilizing data analytics can help identify at-risk students and personalize interventions to meet their specific needs (Topol, 2019).

Increased Funding and Support

Advocacy efforts can lead to increased funding and policy support for school-based mental health programs.

- **Government Initiatives**: Continued advocacy can encourage federal and state governments to allocate more resources to mental health initiatives in schools.
- **Private Sector Partnerships**: Collaborations with private companies and philanthropic organizations can provide additional funding and resources.
- **Community Engagement**: Mobilizing community support can generate local funding and resources for mental health programs (Children's Mental Health Campaign, 2018).

Research and Data

Ongoing research can provide valuable insights into the effectiveness of mental health programs and inform policy decisions.

- **Evidence-Based Practices**: Research can identify and promote evidence-based practices that effectively support student mental health.
- **Program Evaluation**: Regular evaluation of mental health programs can help refine and improve their impact.
- **Data Sharing**: Sharing data and best practices across schools and districts can facilitate the adoption of successful mental health interventions (Mellin, Taylor, & Weist, 2011).

Global Collaboration

International collaboration can enhance the development and implementation of effective mental health policies in schools.

- **Sharing Best Practices**: Learning from successful programs in other countries can inform the development of effective mental health initiatives.
- **Collaborative Research**: International research partnerships can advance the understanding of mental health issues and effective interventions.
- **Policy Alignment**: Aligning policies with international standards can improve the consistency and quality of mental health support in schools (World Health Organization, 2020).

The future of mental health in education presents both challenges and opportunities. Addressing resource limitations, reducing stigma, and closing policy gaps are essential steps for improving mental health support in schools. At the same time, leveraging technological innovations, securing increased funding, advancing research, and fostering global collaboration can create a supportive and inclusive environment for all students. By working together, educators, policymakers, mental health professionals, and communities can ensure that mental health becomes an integral part of the education system, promoting the well-being and success of every student.

CONCLUDING THOUGHTS

Mental health in education is a critical issue that impacts the well-being, academic performance, and future success of students worldwide. Throughout this book, we have explored various aspects of mental health in educational settings, including understanding mental health disorders, identifying and addressing these issues, the role of parents and guardians, professional development for educators, implementing school-based mental health programs, crisis management, leveraging technology, and the importance of policy and advocacy. In this concluding chapter, I will summarize the key points discussed and provide policy recommendations for countries, schools, and communities to adopt.

Summary of Key Points

Understanding Mental Health in Education

Mental health is a vital component of overall health and significantly influences learning and academic achievement. Students with untreated mental health disorders are at a higher risk of poor academic performance, absenteeism, and dropping out of school. Common mental health issues among students include anxiety, depression, ADHD, and conduct disorders. Early identification and intervention are crucial for mitigating these risks and supporting student success.

Identifying and Addressing Mental Health Issues

Educators, parents, and peers play an essential role in recognizing the signs of mental health issues. Schools can utilize screening tools and comprehensive assessments to identify students in need of support. Effective intervention strategies include counseling services, behavioral interventions, and academic accommodations. Creating a supportive school environment that promotes well-being and addresses home-based stressors is also critical.

The Role of Parents and Guardians

Parents and guardians are integral to supporting their children's mental health. Engaging parents in mental health initiatives, recognizing and addressing home-based stressors, maintaining effective communication with teachers, and utilizing available resources can create a supportive environment that fosters well-being and academic success. Real-life examples of parental involvement demonstrate the positive impact of a strong support system.

Professional Development for Educators

Professional development for educators is essential for equipping them with the skills and knowledge to support students' mental health. Training in mental health awareness, stress management, and resilience can enhance teachers' ability to identify and address mental health issues. Self-care strategies and building a resilient educational workforce are also important for maintaining educators' well-being.

Implementing School-Based Mental Health Programs

School-based mental health programs provide accessible support for students and create a comprehensive approach to mental health. Key components of successful programs include needs assessment, collaboration with mental health professionals, funding and sustainability, and ongoing evaluation. Examples of successful programs highlight the importance of a holistic approach that integrates prevention, intervention, and intensive support.

Crisis Management and Intervention

Effective crisis management and intervention are crucial for ensuring the safety and well-being of students and staff. Developing crisis response plans, handling mental health emergencies, providing post-crisis support, and collaborating with community resources are essential components. Lessons learned from past crises underscore the importance of preparedness, immediate support, and long-term recovery efforts.

Leveraging Technology for Mental Health Support

Technology offers innovative solutions for supporting mental health in educational settings. Telehealth services, mental health apps, online counseling, support groups, and social media can enhance access to resources and provide flexible support options. Emerging trends such as AI, VR therapy, data analytics, and gamification hold promise for further improving mental health outcomes.

Policy and Advocacy for Mental Health in Education

Policy and advocacy are critical for advancing mental health support in schools. Effective policies, increased funding, and strong advocacy efforts can drive positive change. International perspectives provide valuable insights into successful approaches, and future opportunities include leveraging technology, securing funding, advancing research, and fostering global collaboration.

Policy Recommendations

To effectively address mental health in education, countries, schools, and communities should adopt comprehensive and evidence-based policies. The following policy recommendations aim to guide the development and implementation of mental health support systems in educational settings.

National and State-Level Policies

1. Implement Comprehensive Mental Health Education

Mandate mental health education as part of the national curriculum to raise awareness and reduce stigma. This education should cover common mental health issues, coping strategies, and available resources. Integrating mental health education from early childhood through high school ensures that students develop an understanding of mental health and are equipped with skills to manage their own well-being and support their peers.

- **Curriculum Integration**: Mental health topics should be included in subjects like health education, science, and social studies.
- **Teacher Training**: Provide professional development for educators to effectively teach mental health topics.
- **Resource Development**: Develop age-appropriate educational materials and resources for students and teachers.

1. **Increase Funding for School-Based Mental Health Services**

Allocate sufficient funding to hire trained mental health professionals, such as counselors, psychologists, and social workers, in schools. Ensure that funding is sustained and prioritized in education budgets to maintain and expand mental health services.

- **Budget Allocation**: Governments should allocate a specific percentage of the education budget to mental health services.
- **Grants and Incentives**: Provide grants and financial incentives to schools that implement comprehensive mental health programs.
- **Public-Private Partnerships**: Encourage collaborations with private sector organizations to fund mental health initiatives.

1. **Standardize Mental Health Screening and Assessment**

Develop and implement standardized screening tools and assessment protocols to identify students in need of mental health support. Regularly review and update these tools based on the latest research and best practices.

- **Universal Screening**: Implement regular mental health screenings for all students to identify those at risk.
- **Training for Staff**: Train school staff to administer screenings and interpret results accurately.
- **Referral Systems**: Establish clear referral pathways for students identified as needing additional support.

Support Telehealth and Technology Integration

Promote the use of telehealth services and mental health apps to enhance access to care, especially in underserved areas. Provide schools with the necessary infrastructure and training to integrate these technologies effectively.

- **Telehealth Platforms**: Invest in secure telehealth platforms that comply with privacy regulations.
- **Digital Literacy**: Ensure students, parents, and staff are trained to use telehealth and mental health apps.
- **Access to Technology**: Provide devices and internet access to students and families who need them.

1. **Establish Crisis Response Protocols**

Develop national and state-level guidelines for crisis management in schools to ensure a coordinated and effective response to mental health emergencies.

- **Crisis Teams**: Form multidisciplinary crisis response teams in schools.
- **Crisis Drills**: Conduct regular drills and simulations to prepare for different types of crises.
- **Community Resources**: Collaborate with local mental health agencies and emergency services for crisis intervention.

School-Level Policies

1. Create a Supportive School Climate

Develop policies that promote a positive and inclusive school climate. Implement anti-bullying programs, encourage student voice and participation, and foster a culture of respect and empathy.

- **Anti-Bullying Initiatives**: Enforce strict anti-bullying policies and provide support for victims.
- **Student Councils**: Establish student councils to give students a platform to voice their concerns and suggestions.
- **Cultural Competency Training**: Provide training to staff and students on diversity, equity, and inclusion.

1. Integrate Social and Emotional Learning (SEL)

Incorporate SEL programs into the school curriculum to help students develop essential skills for managing emotions, building relationships, and making responsible decisions.

- **Curriculum Development**: Integrate SEL into daily lessons and activities.
- **Professional Development**: Train teachers to deliver SEL programs effectively.
- **Assessment and Evaluation**: Regularly assess the impact of SEL programs on student outcomes.

1. Provide Accessible Mental Health Services

Ensure that mental health services are readily available to all students. Create private and safe spaces for counseling and support services within the school.

- **Counseling Centers**: Establish dedicated counseling centers in schools.
- **Confidentiality**: Ensure that all mental health services maintain strict confidentiality.

1. **Engage Parents and Guardians**

Develop strategies to actively involve parents and guardians in mental health initiatives. Offer workshops, resources, and regular communication to support their involvement.

- **Parent Workshops**: Conduct workshops on mental health awareness and strategies to support children at home.
- **Regular Updates**: Provide parents with regular updates on their child's progress and available resources.
- **Parent Support Groups**: Create support groups for parents to share experiences and gain support.

1. **Monitor and Evaluate Programs**

Regularly evaluate the effectiveness of mental health programs and interventions. Use data to inform continuous improvement and ensure that services meet the needs of students.

- **Data Collection**: Collect data on program outcomes, including student well-being and academic performance.
- **Feedback Mechanisms**: Implement feedback mechanisms to gather input from students, parents, and staff.

- **Continuous Improvement**: Use evaluation results to refine and improve mental health programs.

1. **Support Staff Well-Being**

Implement policies that support the mental health and well-being of school staff. Provide access to mental health resources, promote work-life balance, and encourage a supportive work environment.

- **Employee Assistance Programs**: Offer programs that provide counseling and support for staff.
- **Professional Development**: Provide training on stress management and self-care.
- **Wellness Initiatives**: Develop wellness initiatives, such as fitness programs and mental health days.

Addressing mental health in schools requires a holistic approach that includes prevention, early identification, intervention, and continuous support. A comprehensive strategy should involve:

- **Preventative Education**: Educating students about mental health from an early age to build resilience and promote healthy coping mechanisms.

- **Early Identification**: Training teachers and staff to recognize the early signs of mental health issues and take appropriate action.

- **Intervention Programs**: Implementing evidence-based interventions that address the specific needs of students.
- **Continuous Support**: Providing ongoing support to students through counseling, peer support groups, and access to mental health resources.

Community-Level Policies

1. Raise Awareness and Reduce Stigma

Conduct public awareness campaigns to educate the community about mental health issues and the importance of mental health support in schools. Use media, social media, and community events to disseminate information.

- **Public Campaigns**: Launch campaigns to promote mental health awareness and reduce stigma.
- **Media Engagement**: Work with local media to cover mental health topics and initiatives.
- **Community Events**: Organize events such as mental health fairs and awareness walks.

1. Build Community Partnerships

Establish strong partnerships between schools, local mental health agencies, healthcare providers, and community organizations. Collaborate on initiatives and share resources to support student mental health.

- **Collaborative Networks**: Create networks that facilitate collaboration between schools and community organizations.
- **Resource Sharing**: Share resources and expertise to enhance mental health services.
- **Joint Initiatives**: Develop joint initiatives to address community-specific mental health needs.

1. Provide Financial Assistance for Families

Offer financial assistance programs to support families in accessing mental health services. Address economic barriers that may prevent students from receiving the care they need.

- **Subsidies and Grants**: Provide subsidies and grants to families for mental health services.
- **Sliding Scale Fees**: Implement sliding scale fees for services based on family income.
- **Community Funds**: Establish community funds to support families in need.

1. **Promote Safe and Supportive Environments**

Work with community organizations to create safe and supportive environments for children and adolescents. Address issues such as housing instability, food insecurity, and exposure to violence.

- **Safety Programs**: Develop programs that address safety and security in the community.
- **Basic Needs Support**: Provide support for basic needs, such as housing and food.
- **Violence Prevention**: Implement violence prevention programs and support services for victims.

1. **Encourage Volunteerism and Peer Support**

Foster a culture of volunteerism and peer support within the community. Encourage community members to get involved in mentoring, tutoring, and providing emotional support to students.

- **Mentorship Programs**: Develop mentorship programs that connect students with positive role models.

- **Volunteer Networks**: Create networks of volunteers to support school-based initiatives.
- **Peer Support Groups**: Establish peer support groups for students to share experiences and support each other.

The integration of mental health support within the education system is not just a necessity but a foundational element that determines the overall development and success of students. As we look towards the future, it is imperative to adopt a holistic and collaborative approach to mental health in education. This concluding section summarizes key perspectives and provides a forward-looking view on policy recommendations that can be adopted globally to foster a supportive educational environment for mental health.

Collaboration and Community Involvement

Effective mental health support extends beyond the classroom and involves the entire community. Collaboration between schools, parents, mental health professionals, and community organizations is essential for creating a supportive network for students.

- **Parental Engagement**: Actively involving parents in mental health initiatives can reinforce the support system at home and ensure a cohesive approach to addressing mental health issues.

- **Community Resources**: Leveraging community resources, such as local mental health agencies and support groups, can enhance the support available to students and families.

- **Professional Development**: Providing continuous professional development for educators and staff ensures that they are equipped with the latest knowledge and skills to support student mental health effectively.

- **Leveraging Technology for Enhanced Support**

Technology plays a pivotal role in modernizing mental health support in education. The integration of telehealth services, mental health apps, and online counseling platforms can significantly improve access to care and provide flexible support options for students.

- **Telehealth Services**: Expanding telehealth services allows students to receive mental health support remotely, breaking down geographical barriers and making it easier for students in underserved areas to access care.

- **Mental Health Apps**: Utilizing mental health apps can provide students with tools for managing stress, tracking their moods, and accessing immediate support. These apps can be integrated into the school's mental health program to complement traditional services.

- **Online Counseling Platforms**: Online platforms for counseling can offer flexible scheduling and privacy, encouraging students who might be hesitant to seek help in person to access support.

- **Global Collaboration and Policy Alignment**

Countries can learn from each other's successes and challenges in implementing mental health policies in education. By sharing best practices and aligning policies with international standards, we can create a more consistent and effective approach to mental health support in schools worldwide.

- **Sharing Best Practices**: Countries that have successfully integrated mental health support in schools can share their strategies and frameworks with others. International conferences, workshops, and publications can facilitate this exchange of knowledge.

- **Policy Alignment**: Aligning national policies with international standards and guidelines, such as those provided by the World Health Organization, can ensure a high level of consistency and quality in mental health services across different regions.

- **Collaborative Research**: Engaging in collaborative research projects with international partners can advance our understanding of mental health issues and effective interventions in educational settings.

Future Opportunities and Innovations

Looking forward, several opportunities and innovations hold promise for advancing mental health support in education:

- **Artificial Intelligence (AI)**: AI can be used to develop predictive models that identify students at risk of mental health issues, allowing for early intervention. AI-driven chatbots can also provide immediate support and resources to students in need.

- **Virtual Reality (VR) Therapy**: VR can offer immersive experiences for therapeutic interventions, such as exposure therapy for anxiety and PTSD. VR environments can be used to create safe spaces for students to practice coping skills.

- **Gamification**: Incorporating game design elements into mental health programs can increase student engagement and motivation. Games can teach coping strategies, emotional regulation, and resilience in an interactive and enjoyable way.

- **Data Analytics**: Utilizing data analytics can help schools track the effectiveness of mental health programs and make data-driven decisions to improve services. Regular analysis of data can identify trends and areas for improvement.

Policy Recommendations for Global Adoption

To effectively support mental health in education, the following policy recommendations should be considered for global adoption:

- **Comprehensive Mental Health Education**: Integrate mental health education into the national curriculum across all grade levels. This should include teaching about common mental health issues, coping strategies, and where to seek help.

- **Increased Funding**: Governments should allocate sufficient and sustained funding for school-based mental health services, ensuring that all students have access to trained mental health professionals.

- **Standardized Screening and Assessment**: Implement standardized mental health screening and assessment tools in schools, with regular updates based on the latest research and best practices.

- ## Support for Telehealth and Technology Integration

Promote the use of telehealth services and mental health apps to enhance access to care, especially in underserved areas. Provide schools with the necessary infrastructure and training to integrate these technologies effectively.

- **Telehealth Platforms**: Invest in secure telehealth platforms that comply with privacy regulations. These platforms should be easy to use and accessible to students, parents, and school staff. Ensuring robust cybersecurity measures is critical to protect sensitive information.

- **Digital Literacy**: Ensure students, parents, and staff are trained to use telehealth and mental health apps. Offer training sessions to help users become comfortable with the technology and understand how to access and utilize mental health resources effectively.

- **Access to Technology**: Provide devices and internet access to students and families who need them. Implement programs to distribute tablets, laptops, and internet hotspots to ensure that all students can benefit from telehealth services and online mental health resources.

- ## Establish Crisis Response Protocols

Develop national and state-level guidelines for crisis management in schools to ensure a coordinated and effective response to mental health emergencies.

Crisis Teams: Form multidisciplinary crisis response teams in schools that include administrators, counselors, psychologists, social workers, and local emergency responders. These teams should be trained in crisis intervention and response.

Crisis Drills: Conduct regular drills and simulations to prepare for different types of crises, including mental health emergencies. These drills help ensure that all staff and students are familiar with the procedures and can act swiftly and appropriately.

Community Resources: Collaborate with local mental health agencies and emergency services for crisis intervention. Establish strong relationships with community resources to ensure that schools can quickly access additional support when needed.

School-Level Policies

• Create a Supportive School Climate

Develop policies that promote a positive and inclusive school climate. Implement anti-bullying programs, encourage student voice and participation, and foster a culture of respect and empathy.

- **Anti-Bullying Initiatives**: Enforce strict anti-bullying policies and provide support for victims. Create anonymous reporting systems and ensure that all incidents are thoroughly investigated and addressed.

- **Student Councils**: Establish student councils to give students a platform to voice their concerns and suggestions. These councils can play a critical role in developing and implementing mental health initiatives.

- **Cultural Competency Training**: Provide training to staff and students on diversity, equity, and inclusion. Promote understanding and respect for different cultures, backgrounds, and perspectives.

• Integrate Social and Emotional Learning (SEL)

Incorporate SEL programs into the school curriculum to help students develop essential skills for managing emotions, building relationships, and making responsible decisions.

- **Curriculum Development**: Integrate SEL into daily lessons and activities. Use evidence-based SEL programs and materials to teach skills such as empathy, self-regulation, and conflict resolution.

- **Professional Development**: Train teachers to deliver SEL programs effectively. Provide ongoing support and resources to help educators incorporate SEL into their teaching practices.

- **Assessment and Evaluation**: Regularly assess the impact of SEL programs on student outcomes. Use data to refine and improve SEL initiatives.

- **Provide Accessible Mental Health Services**

Ensure that mental health services are readily available to all students. Create private and safe spaces for counseling and support services within the school.

- **Counseling Centers**: Establish dedicated counseling centers in schools. These centers should be welcoming and confidential, providing a safe space for students to seek help.

- **Confidentiality**: Ensure that all mental health services maintain strict confidentiality. Protect students' privacy to encourage them to seek help without fear of judgment or stigma.

- **Outreach Programs**: Develop outreach programs to inform students about available mental health resources. Use posters, announcements, and social media to promote services and reduce stigma.

- **Engage Parents and Guardians**

Develop strategies to actively involve parents and guardians in mental health initiatives. Offer workshops, resources, and regular communication to support their involvement.

Parent Workshops: Conduct workshops on mental health awareness and strategies to support children at home. Provide practical tips and resources to help parents understand and address their children's mental health needs.

Regular Updates: Provide parents with regular updates on their child's progress and available resources. Use newsletters, emails, and parent-teacher conferences to keep parents informed.

Parent Support Groups: Create support groups for parents to share experiences and gain support. Facilitate connections between parents facing similar challenges and provide a platform for mutual support.

- **Monitor and Evaluate Programs**

Regularly evaluate the effectiveness of mental health programs and interventions. Use data to inform continuous improvement and ensure that services meet the needs of students.

Data Collection: Collect data on program outcomes, including student well-being and academic performance. Use surveys, assessments, and feedback forms to gather information on the effectiveness of mental health initiatives.

Feedback Mechanisms: Implement feedback mechanisms to gather input from students, parents, and staff. Regularly review feedback to identify areas for improvement and ensure that the programs are meeting their objectives.

Continuous Improvement: Use evaluation results to refine and enhance mental health programs. Share successful strategies and best practices across schools and districts to promote a culture of continuous improvement.

It is clear that fostering a supportive and inclusive environment within our schools is not just beneficial but essential for the holistic development of students. By implementing comprehensive policies, securing adequate funding, and leveraging innovative technologies, we can ensure that mental health becomes a cornerstone of our educational systems. Collaboration among educators, policymakers, mental health professionals, parents, and communities will pave the way for creating resilient, empowered, and healthy future generations. Let us commit to making mental health support an integral part of education, recognizing that the well-being of our students today shapes the promise of our society tomorrow. Together, we can build a brighter, healthier future for all.

References

Adelman, H. S., & Taylor, L. (2006). The school leader's guide to student learning supports: New directions for addressing barriers to learning. Thousand Oaks, CA: Corwin Press.

American Academy of Pediatrics. (2019). Policy statement: School-based mental health services. *Pediatrics, 144*(6), e20192775. doi:10.1542/peds.2019-2775

American Federation of Teachers. (2017). 2017 Educator Quality of Work Life Survey. Retrieved from https://www.aft.org/sites/default/files/ 2017_eqwl_survey_web.pdf

American Psychiatric Association. (2013). Diagnostic and statistical manual of mental disorders (5th ed.). Arlington, VA: American Psychiatric Publishing. Retrieved from https://www.psychiatry.org/psychiatrists/practice/dsm

American Psychiatric Association. (2013). Diagnostic and statistical manual of mental disorders (5th ed.). Arlington, VA: American Psychiatric Publishing. Retrieved from https://www.psychiatry.org/psychiatrists/practice/dsm

American Psychological Association. (2013). Telepsychology guidelines. Retrieved from https://www.apa.org/practice/guidelines/telepsychology[1]

American Psychological Association. (2020). Stress in America 2020: A National Mental Health Crisis. Retrieved

---

1. https://www.apa.org/practice/guidelines/telepsychology

from   https://www.apa.org/news/press/releases/stress/2020/report-october[2]

Baker, T., & Ray, M. (2011). Online mental health services: Outreach, engagement, and ethical issues. *Journal of Technology in Human Services, 29*(4), 263-276. doi:10.1080/15228835.2011.639931

Barak, A., Hen, L., Boniel-Nissim, M., & Shapira, N. (2008). A comprehensive review and a meta-analysis of the effectiveness of internet-based psychotherapeutic interventions. *Journal of Technology in Human Services, 26*(2-4), 109-160. doi:10.1080/15228830802094429

Basch, C. E. (2011). Physical activity and the achievement gap among urban minority youth. *Journal of School Health, 81*(10), 626-634. doi:10.1111/j.1746-1561.2011.00637.x

Berthelsen, D., & Walker, S. (2008). Parents' involvement in their children's education. *Family Matters, 79,* 34-41.

Brock, S. E., Nickerson, A. B., Reeves, M. A., Jimerson, S. R., Lieberman, R., & Feinberg, T. (2009). *School Crisis Prevention and Intervention: The PREPaRE Model.* Bethesda, MD: National Association of School Psychologists. Retrieved from https://www.nasponline.org[3]

Brock, S. E., Nickerson, A. B., Reeves, M. A., Jimerson, S. R., Lieberman, R., & Feinberg, T. (2009). School Crisis Prevention and Intervention: The PREPaRE Model. Bethesda, MD: National Association of School Psychologists. Retrieved from https://www.nasponline.org[4]

2. https://www.apa.org/news/press/releases/stress/2020/report-october

3. https://www.nasponline.org

Centers for Disease Control and Prevention. (2020). Mental health-related emergency department visits among children aged <18 years during the COVID-19 pandemic – United States, January 1–October 17, 2020. Retrieved from https://www.cdc.gov/mmwr/volumes/69/wr/mm6945a3.htm[5]

Centers for Disease Control and Prevention. (2020). Mental health-related emergency department visits among children aged <18 years during the COVID-19 pandemic – United States, January 1–October 17, 2020. Retrieved from https://www.cdc.gov/mmwr/volumes/69/wr/mm6945a3.htm[6]

Children's Mental Health Campaign. (2018). Advocacy toolkit. Retrieved from https://www.childrensmentalhealthcampaign.org[7]

Conners, C. K. (2008). Conners Comprehensive Behavior Rating Scales (CBRS). Toronto, Ontario, Canada: Multi-Health Systems.

Corrigan, P. W., Druss, B. G., & Perlick, D. A. (2014). The impact of mental illness stigma on seeking and participating in mental health care. *Psychological Science in the Public Interest, 15*(2), 37-70. doi:10.1177/1529100614531398

Cowan, K. C., Vaillancourt, K., Rossen, E., & Pollitt, K. (2013). A Framework for Safe and Successful Schools.

---

4. https://www.nasponline.org

5. https://www.cdc.gov/mmwr/volumes/69/wr/mm6945a3.htm

6. https://www.cdc.gov/mmwr/volumes/69/wr/mm6945a3.htm

7. https://www.childrensmentalhealthcampaign.org

National Association of School Psychologists. Retrieved from https://www.nasponline.org/resources-and-publications/ resources-and-podcasts/school-climate-safety-and-crisis/a-framework-for-safe-and-successful-schools

Dorado, J. S., Martinez, M., McArthur, L. E., & Leibovitz, T. (2016). Healthy Environments and Response to Trauma in Schools (HEARTS): A whole-school, multi-level, prevention and intervention program for creating trauma-informed, safe and supportive schools. *School Mental Health, 8*(1), 163-176. doi:10.1007/ s12310-016-9177-0

Durlak, J. A., Weissberg, R. P., Dymnicki, A. B., Taylor, R. D., & Schellinger, K. B. (2011). The impact of enhancing students' social and emotional learning: A meta-analysis of school-based universal interventions. *Child Development, 82*(1), 405-432. doi:10.1111/j.1467-8624.2010.01564.x

Durlak, J. A., Weissberg, R. P., Dymnicki, A. B., Taylor, R. D., & Schellinger, K. B. (2011). The impact of enhancing students' social and emotional learning: A meta-analysis of school-based universal interventions. *Child Development, 82*(1), 405-432. doi:10.1111/j.1467-8624.2010.01564.x

Durlak, J. A., Weissberg, R. P., Dymnicki, A. B., Taylor, R. D., & Schellinger, K. B. (2011). The impact of enhancing students' social and emotional learning: A meta-analysis of school-based universal interventions. *Child Development, 82*(1), 405-432. doi:10.1111/j.1467-8624.2010.01564.x

Durlak, J. A., Weissberg, R. P., Dymnicki, A. B., Taylor, R. D., & Schellinger, K. B. (2011). The impact of enhancing students' social and emotional learning: A meta-analysis of school-based universal interventions. *Child Development, 82*(1), 405-432. doi:10.1111/j.1467-8624.2010.01564.x

Durlak, J. A., Weissberg, R. P., Dymnicki, A. B., Taylor, R. D., & Schellinger, K. B. (2011). The impact of enhancing students' social and emotional learning: A meta-analysis of school-based universal interventions. *Child Development, 82*(1), 405-432. doi:10.1111/j.1467-8624.2010.01564.x

Durlak, J. A., Weissberg, R. P., Dymnicki, A. B., Taylor, R. D., & Schellinger, K. B. (2011). The impact of enhancing students' social and emotional learning: A meta-analysis of school-based universal interventions. *Child Development, 82*(1), 405-432. doi:10.1111/j.1467-8624.2010.01564.x

EdWeek Research Center. (2020). Student Mental Health During COVID-19: How the Pandemic Has Impacted Student Well-Being. Retrieved from https://www.edweek.org/leadership/student-mental-health-during-covid-19-how-the-pandemic-has-impacted-student-well-being/2020/09

Epstein, J. L. (2011). School, family, and community partnerships: Preparing educators and improving schools. Boulder, CO: Westview Press.

Farmer, E. M., Burns, B. J., Phillips, S. D., Angold, A., & Costello, E. J. (2003). Pathways into and through mental health services for children and adolescents. *Psychiatric Services, 54*(1), 60-66. doi:10.1176/appi.ps.54.1.60

Fazel, M., Hoagwood, K., Stephan, S., & Ford, T. (2014). Mental health interventions in schools in high-income countries. *The Lancet Psychiatry, 1*(5), 377-387. doi:10.1016/S2215-0366(14)70312-8

Fazel, M., Hoagwood, K., Stephan, S., & Ford, T. (2014). Mental health interventions in schools in high-income countries. *The Lancet Psychiatry, 1*(5), 377-387. doi:10.1016/S2215-0366(14)70312-8

Fitzpatrick, K. K., Darcy, A., & Vierhile, M. (2017). Delivering cognitive behavior therapy to young adults with symptoms of depression and anxiety using a fully automated conversational agent (Woebot): A randomized controlled trial. *JMIR Mental Health, 4*(2), e19. doi:10.2196/mental.7785

García, E., & Weiss, E. (2020). COVID-19 and student performance, equity, and U.S. education policy: Lessons from pre-pandemic research to inform relief, recovery, and rebuilding. *Economic Policy Institute*. Retrieved from https://www.epi.org/publication/the-consequences-of-the-covid-19-pandemic-for-education-performance-and-equity-in-the-united-states-what-can-we-learn-from-pre-pandemic-research-to-inform-relief-recovery-and-rebuilding/

Gay, G. (2010). Culturally responsive teaching: Theory, research, and practice. New York, NY: Teachers College Press.

Gay, G. (2010). Culturally responsive teaching: Theory, research, and practice. New York, NY: Teachers College Press.

Glasheen, K., Shochet, I., & Campbell, M. (2016). Online mental health resources for adolescents: The role of social networks. *Social Work in Health Care, 55*(3), 235-253. doi:10.1080/00981389.2015.1125382

Golberstein, E., Wen, H., & Miller, B. F. (2020). Coronavirus Disease 2019 (COVID-19) and Mental Health for Children and Adolescents. *JAMA Pediatrics, 174*(9), 819-820. doi:10.1001/jamapediatrics.2020.1456

Goodman, R. (2001). Psychometric properties of the strengths and difficulties questionnaire. *Journal of the American Academy of Child & Adolescent Psychiatry, 40*(11), 1337-1345. doi:10.1097/00004583-200111000-00015

Goodman, R. (2001). Psychometric properties of the strengths and difficulties questionnaire. *Journal of the American Academy of Child & Adolescent Psychiatry, 40*(11), 1337-1345. doi:10.1097/00004583-200111000-00015

Griffiths, K. M., Calear, A. L., Banfield, M., & Tam, A. (2009). Systematic review on Internet Support Groups (ISGs) and their use in depression and anxiety. *Journal of Medical Internet Research, 11*(3), e40. doi:10.2196/jmir.1270

Gros, D. F., Morland, L. A., Greene, C. J., Acierno, R., Strachan, M., Egede, L., ... & Frueh, B. C. (2013). Delivery of evidence-based psychotherapy via video telehealth. *Journal of Psychopathology and Behavioral Assessment, 35*(4), 506-521. doi:10.1007/s10862-013-9363-4

Guo, J. J., Wade, T. J., Pan, W., & Keller, K. N. (2008). School-based health centers: Cost-benefit analysis and impact on health care disparities. *American Journal of Public Health,* *98*(9), 1615-1622. doi:10.2105/AJPH.2007.120320

Guo, J. J., Wade, T. J., Pan, W., & Keller, K. N. (2008). School-based health centers: Cost-benefit analysis and impact on health care disparities. *American Journal of Public Health,* *98*(9), 1615-1622. doi:10.2105/AJPH.2007.120320

Harris, B. (2020). Digital mental health: The answer to the global mental health crisis? *The Lancet Digital Health,* *2*(10), e493-e494. doi:10.1016/S2589-7500(20)30189-0

Heath, M. A., Ryan, K., Dean, B., & Bingham, R. (2007). History of school shootings in the United States: Implications for counseling school violence survivors. *Journal of School Violence,* *6*(1), 27-52. doi:10.1300/J202v06n01_03

Hoagwood, K., Olin, S. S., Kerker, B. D., Kratochwill, T. R., Crowe, M., & Saka, N. (2007). Empirically based school interventions targeted at academic and mental health functioning. *Journal of Emotional and Behavioral Disorders,* *15*(2), 66-92. doi:10.1177/10634266070150020301

Hoover, S. A., Lever, N., Sachdev, N., & Brindis, C. D. (2017). Advancing comprehensive school mental health: Guidance from the field. *Adolescent Psychiatry,* *7*(2), 142-153. doi:10.2174/2210676607021706221206

Individuals with Disabilities Education Act (IDEA). (1975). Education for All Handicapped Children Act. Retrieved from https://sites.ed.gov/idea/

Jain, B. (2021). A Psychiatric Walk-In Model Providing Immediate Access for Patients Across the Lifespan.

Jennings, P. A., & Greenberg, M. T. (2009). The prosocial classroom: Teacher social and emotional competence in relation to student and classroom outcomes. *Review of Educational Research, 79*(1), 491-525. doi:10.3102/0034654308325693

Jennings, P. A., & Greenberg, M. T. (2009). The prosocial classroom: Teacher social and emotional competence in relation to student and classroom outcomes. *Review of Educational Research, 79*(1), 491-525. doi:10.3102/0034654308325693

Johnson, D., Deterding, S., Kuhn, K. A., Staneva, A., Stoyanov, S., & Hides, L. (2016). Gamification for health and wellbeing: A systematic review of the literature. *Internet Interventions, 6,* 89-106. doi:10.1016/j.invent.2016.10.002

Kessler, R. C., Foster, C. L., Saunders, W. B., & Stang, P. E. (1995). Social consequences of psychiatric disorders, I: Educational attainment. *American Journal of Psychiatry, 152*(7), 1026-1032. doi:10.1176/ajp.152.7.1026

Kessler, R. C., Foster, C. L., Saunders, W. B., & Stang, P. E. (1995). Social consequences of psychiatric disorders, I: Educational attainment. *American Journal of Psychiatry, 152*(7), 1026-1032. doi:10.1176/ajp.152.7.1026

Kim, L. E., & Asbury, K. (2020). 'Like a rug had been pulled from under you': The impact of COVID-19 on teachers in England during the first six weeks of the UK lockdown.

British Journal of Educational Psychology, 90(4), 1062-1083. doi:10.1111/bjep.12381

Kovacs, M. (1992). Children's Depression Inventory (CDI). Toronto, Ontario, Canada: Multi-Health Systems.

Kroenke, K., Spitzer, R. L., & Williams, J. B. (2001). The PHQ-9: Validity of a brief depression severity measure. *Journal of General Internal Medicine, 16*(9), 606-613. doi:10.1046/j.1525-1497.2001.016009606.x

Kroenke, K., Spitzer, R. L., & Williams, J. B. (2001). The PHQ-9: Validity of a brief depression severity measure. *Journal of General Internal Medicine, 16*(9), 606-613. doi:10.1046/j.1525-1497.2001.016009606.x

Kronenberg, M. E., Osofsky, H. J., Osofsky, J. D., Many, M., Hardy, M., & Arey, J. (2010). First responder culture: Implications for mental health professionals providing services following a natural disaster. *Psychiatry: Interpersonal and Biological Processes, 73*(3), 283-297. doi:10.1521/psyc.2010.73.3.283

Kumar, S. (2015). Mobile health: Revolutionizing healthcare through technology. *BMJ Innovations, 1*(1), 1-4. doi:10.1136/bmjinnov-2014-000003

Kumar, S. (2015). Mobile health: Revolutionizing healthcare through technology. *BMJ Innovations, 1*(1), 1-4. doi:10.1136/bmjinnov-2014-000003

Kutcher, S., & Wei, Y. (2013). Challenges and solutions in the implementation of the school-based pathway to care model: The lessons from Nova Scotia and beyond.

Canadian Journal of School Psychology, 28(1), 90-102. doi:10.1177/0829573512468859

Kutcher, S., & Wei, Y. (2013). Challenges and solutions in the implementation of the school-based pathway to care model: The lessons from Nova Scotia and beyond. *Canadian Journal of School Psychology, 28*(1), 90-102. doi:10.1177/0829573512468859

Kutcher, S., & Wei, Y. (2013). Challenges and solutions in the implementation of the school-based pathway to care model: The lessons from Nova Scotia and beyond. *Canadian Journal of School Psychology, 28*(1), 90-102. doi:10.1177/0829573512468859

Kutcher, S., & Wei, Y. (2013). Challenges and solutions in the implementation of the school-based pathway to care model: The lessons from Nova Scotia and beyond. *Canadian Journal of School Psychology, 28*(1), 90-102. doi:10.1177/0829573512468859

Leeb, R. T., Bitsko, R. H., Radhakrishnan, L., Martinez, P., Njai, R., & Holland, K. M. (2020). Mental health-related emergency department visits among children aged <18 years during the COVID-19 pandemic – United States, January 1–October 17, 2020. *MMWR. Morbidity and Mortality Weekly Report, 69*(45), 1675-1680. doi:10.15585/ mmwr.mm6945a3

Leeb, R. T., Bitsko, R. H., Radhakrishnan, L., Martinez, P., Njai, R., & Holland, K. M. (2020). Mental health-related emergency department visits among children aged <18 years during the COVID-19 pandemic – United States, January

1–October 17, 2020. *MMWR. Morbidity and Mortality Weekly Report, 69*(45), 1675-1680. doi:10.15585/mmwr.mm6945a3

Levitt, J. M., Saka, N., Romanelli, L. H., & Hoagwood, K. (2007). Early identification of mental health problems in schools: The status of instrumentation. *Journal of School Psychology, 45*(2), 163-191. doi:10.1016/j.jsp.2006.11.005

Livingstone, S. (2014). Developing social media literacy: How children learn to interpret risky opportunities on social network sites. *Communication & Society, 17*(9), 1023-1039. doi:10.1080/1369118X.2013.870563

Loades, M. E., Chatburn, E., Higson-Sweeney, N., Reynolds, S., Shafran, R., Brigden, A., ... & Crawley, E. (2020). Rapid systematic review: The impact of social isolation and loneliness on the mental health of children and adolescents in the context of COVID-19. *Journal of the American Academy of Child & Adolescent Psychiatry, 59*(11), 1218-1239.e3. doi:10.1016/j.jaac.2020.05.009

Luxton, D. D., McCann, R. A., Bush, N. E., Mishkind, M. C., & Reger, G. M. (2011). mHealth for mental health: Integrating smartphone technology in behavioral healthcare. *Professional Psychology: Research and Practice, 42*(6), 505-512. doi:10.1037/a0024485

Madaus, J. W. (2008). Effectiveness of the accommodations process in higher education. *Disability Compliance for Higher Education, 13*(3), 1-8. doi:10.1002/dhe.253

Maples-Keller, J. L., Bunnell, B. E., Kim, S. J., & Rothbaum, B. O. (2017). The use of virtual reality technology in the treatment of anxiety and other psychiatric disorders. *Harvard Review of Psychiatry, 25*(3), 103-113. doi:10.1097/HRP.0000000000000138

Maslach, C., & Leiter, M. P. (2016). Understanding the burnout experience: Recent research and its implications for psychiatry. *World Psychiatry, 15*(2), 103-111. doi:10.1002/wps.20311

Mellin, E. A., Taylor, L., & Weist, M. D. (2011). The expanded school mental health collaboration instrumentation scales: Development and initial psychometrics. *School Mental Health, 3*(2), 95-107. doi:10.1007/s12310-011-9059-4

Mellin, E. A., Taylor, L., & Weist, M. D. (2011). The expanded school mental health collaboration instrumentation scales: Development and initial psychometrics. *School Mental Health, 3*(2), 95-107. doi:10.1007/s12310-011-9059-4

Merikangas, K. R., He, J., Burstein, M., Swendsen, J., Avenevoli, S., Case, B., ... & Olfson, M. (2010). Lifetime prevalence of mental disorders in U.S. adolescents: Results from the National Comorbidity Survey Replication–Adolescent Supplement (NCS-A). *Journal of the American Academy of Child & Adolescent Psychiatry, 49*(10), 980-989. doi:10.1016/j.jaac.2010.05.017

Merikangas, K. R., He, J., Burstein, M., Swendsen, J., Avenevoli, S., Case, B., ... & Olfson, M. (2010). Lifetime prevalence of mental disorders in U.S. adolescents: Results from the National Comorbidity Survey

Replication–Adolescent Supplement (NCS-A). *Journal of the American Academy of Child & Adolescent Psychiatry, 49*(10), 980-989. doi:10.1016/j.jaac.2010.05.017

Mitchell, J. T. (1983). When disaster strikes...The Critical Incident Stress Debriefing process. *Journal of Emergency Medical Services, 8*(1), 36-39. doi:10.3109/07347338308991655

Mojtabai, R., Olfson, M., & Han, B. (2016). National trends in the prevalence and treatment of depression in adolescents and young adults. *Pediatrics, 138*(6), e20161878. doi:10.1542/peds.2016-1878

Mojtabai, R., Olfson, M., & Han, B. (2016). National trends in the prevalence and treatment of depression in adolescents and young adults. *Pediatrics, 138*(6), e20161878. doi:10.1542/peds.2016-1878

Morris, J., & O'Neill, D. (2014). User perceptions of online mental health support: A review of the literature. *Journal of Public Mental Health, 13*(1), 26-39. doi:10.1108/JPMH-04-2013-0026

NAMI. (2021). Mental Health Conditions. Retrieved from https://www.nami.org/About-Mental-Illness/Mental-Health-Conditions

Naslund, J. A., Aschbrenner, K. A., Marsch, L. A., & Bartels, S. J. (2016). The future of mental health care: Peer-to-peer support and social media. *Epidemiology and Psychiatric Sciences, 25*(2), 113-122. doi:10.1017/S2045796015001067

Naslund, J. A., Aschbrenner, K. A., Marsch, L. A., & Bartels, S. J. (2016). The future of mental health care: Peer-to-peer support and social media. *Epidemiology and Psychiatric Sciences, 25*(2), 113-122. doi:10.1017/S2045796015001067

National Alliance on Mental Illness. (2021). Mental health in schools act. Retrieved from https://www.nami.org/Advocacy/Policy-Priorities/Improving-Health/Mental-Health-in-Schools-Act

National Association of School Psychologists. (2016). School psychologists: Providing mental health services to improve the lives and learning of children and youth. Retrieved from https://www.nasponline.org[8]

National Education Association. (2020). Survey: COVID-19 impacting educators' mental health. Retrieved from https://www.nea.org/advocating-for-change/new-from-nea/survey-covid-19-impacting-educators-mental-health

NCTSN. (2006). Psychological First Aid: Field Operations Guide. *National Child Traumatic Stress Network*. Retrieved from https://www.nctsn.org/resources/psychological-first-aid-pfa-field-operations-guide

O'Donnell, D. A., Hawkins, J. D., & McCormick, A. (2008). School mental health services and young children's emotions, behavior, and learning. *Journal of School Health, 78*(1), 6-11. doi:10.1111/j.1746-1561.2007.00258.x

Olweus, D., & Limber, S. P. (2010). Bullying in school: Evaluation and dissemination of the Olweus Bullying

---

Prevention Program. *American Journal of Orthopsychiatry, 80*(1), 124-134. doi:10.1111/j.1939-0025.2010.01015.x

Olweus, D., & Limber, S. P. (2010). Bullying in school: Evaluation and dissemination of the Olweus Bullying Prevention Program. *American Journal of Orthopsychiatry, 80*(1), 124-134. doi:10.1111/j.1939-0025.2010.01015.x

Pressley, T. (2021). Factors contributing to teacher burnout during COVID-19. *Educational Researcher, 50*(5), 325-327. doi:10.3102/0013189X211004138

Reback, R. (2010). Schools' mental health services and young children's emotions, behavior, and learning. *Journal of Policy Analysis and Management, 29*(4), 698-725. doi:10.1002/pam.20528

Reinke, W. M., Stormont, M., Herman, K. C., Puri, R., & Goel, N. (2011). Supporting children's mental health in schools: Teacher perceptions of needs, roles, and barriers. *School Psychology Quarterly, 26*(1), 1-13. doi:10.1037/a0022714

Reupert, A., Greenhalgh, E. M., & Maybery, D. J. (2012). Teachers' experiences of parenting and teaching children with mental health problems: Implications for education and support. *Advances in School Mental Health Promotion, 5*(2), 108-120. doi:10.1080/1754730X.2012.679424

Reupert, A., Greenhalgh, E. M., & Maybery, D. J. (2012). Teachers' experiences of parenting and teaching children with mental health problems: Implications for education and support. *Advances in School Mental Health Promotion, 5*(2), 108-120. doi:10.1080/1754730X.2012.679424

Reynolds, C. R., & Kamphaus, R. W. (2015). Behavioral Assessment System for Children (BASC). Bloomington, MN: Pearson Assessments.

Rigby, K. (2012). Bullying in schools: Addressing desires, not only behaviors. *Educational Psychology Review, 24*(2), 339-348. doi:10.1007/s10648-012-9196-9

Rigby, K. (2012). Bullying in schools: Addressing desires, not only behaviors. *Educational Psychology Review, 24*(2), 339-348. doi:10.1007/s10648-012-9196-9

Rigby, K. (2012). Bullying in schools: Addressing desires, not only behaviors. *Educational Psychology Review, 24*(2), 339-348. doi:10.1007/s10648-012-9196-9

SAMHSA. (2019). Crisis Services: Effectiveness, Cost-Effectiveness, and Funding Strategies. *Substance Abuse and Mental Health Services Administration*. Retrieved from https://www.samhsa.gov/sites/default/files/crisis-services-effectiveness-cost-effectiveness-funding-strategies.pdf

Slee, P. T., Dix, K. L., Lawson, M. J., & Keeves, J. P. (2009). Implementation of a school environment intervention to reduce bullying in early adolescence: The beyond bullying secondary program. *The Australian Journal of Educational & Developmental Psychology, 9*, 32-45.

Spitzer, R. L., Kroenke, K., Williams, J. B., & Löwe, B. (2006). A brief measure for assessing generalized anxiety disorder: The GAD-7. *Archives of Internal Medicine, 166*(10), 1092-1097. doi:10.1001/archinte.166.10.1092

Sugai, G., & Horner, R. H. (2002). The evolution of discipline practices: School-wide positive behavior supports. *Child & Family Behavior Therapy*, *24*(1-2), 23-50. doi:10.1300/J019v24n01_03

Sugai, G., & Horner, R. H. (2002). The evolution of discipline practices: School-wide positive behavior supports. *Child & Family Behavior Therapy*, *24*(1-2), 23-50. doi:10.1300/J019v24n01_03

Thapa, A., Cohen, J., Guffey, S., & Higgins-D'Alessandro, A. (2013). A review of school climate research. *Review of Educational Research*, *83*(3), 357-385. doi:10.3102/0034654313483907

Thapa, A., Cohen, J., Guffey, S., & Higgins-D'Alessandro, A. (2013). A review of school climate research. *Review of Educational Research*, *83*(3), 357-385. doi:10.3102/0034654313483907

Thapa, A., Cohen, J., Guffey, S., & Higgins-D'Alessandro, A. (2013). A review of school climate research. *Review of Educational Research*, *83*(3), 357-385. doi:10.3102/0034654313483907

Topol, E. (2019). High-performance medicine: The convergence of human and artificial intelligence. *Nature Medicine*, *25*(1), 44-56. doi:10.1038/s41591-018-0300-7

Topol, E. (2019). High-performance medicine: The convergence of human and artificial intelligence. *Nature Medicine*, *25*(1), 44-56. doi:10.1038/s41591-018-0300-7

Valkenburg, P. M., Peter, J., & Schouten, A. P. (2006). Friend networking sites and their relationship to adolescents' well-being and social self-esteem. *CyberPsychology & Behavior, 9*(5), 584-590. doi:10.1089/cpb.2006.9.584

Wei, Y., Kutcher, S., & Morgan, C. (2013). Recognizing and responding to adolescent depression in the classroom. *The Professional Counselor, 3*(2), 93-104. doi:10.15241/yw.3.2.93

Weist, M. D., Lever, N. A., Bradshaw, C. P., & Owens, J. S. (2014). Implementation of evidence-based practices in school mental health: A critical review and the way forward. *School Mental Health, 6*(2), 77-89. doi:10.1007/s12310-013-9109-2

Weist, M. D., Lever, N. A., Bradshaw, C. P., & Owens, J. S. (2014). Implementation of evidence-based practices in school mental health: A critical review and the way forward. *School Mental Health, 6*(2), 77-89. doi:10.1007/s12310-013-9109-2

Weist, M. D., Lever, N. A., Bradshaw, C. P., & Owens, J. S. (2014). Implementation of evidence-based practices in school mental health: A critical review and the way forward. *School Mental Health, 6*(2), 77-89. doi:10.1007/s12310-013-9109-2

Weist, M. D., Mellin, E. A., Chambers, K. L., Lever, N. A., Haber, D., & Blaber, C. (2014). Challenges to collaboration in school mental health and strategies for overcoming them.

Journal of School Health, 82(2), 97-105. doi:10.1111/j.1746-1561.2011.00576.x

Weist, M. D., Rubin, M., Moore, E., Adelsheim, S., & Wrobel, G. (2007). Mental health screening in schools. *Journal of School Health, 77*(2), 53-58. doi:10.1111/j.1746-1561.2007.00167.x

Witmer, L. (1909). The psychological clinic. *The Psychological Clinic, 3*(4), 115-128. Retrieved from https://babel.hathitrust.org/cgi/pt?id=mdp.39015076664543

World Health Organization. (2004). Promoting mental health: Concepts, emerging evidence, practice (Summary Report). Geneva: World Health Organization. Retrieved from https://www.who.int/mental_health/evidence/en/promoting_mhh.pdf[9]

World Health Organization. (2020). Mental health and psychosocial considerations during the COVID-19 outbreak. Retrieved from https://www.who.int/docs/default-source/coronaviruse/mental-health-considerations.pdf[10]

World Health Organization. (2021). Adolescent mental health. Retrieved from https://www.who.int/news-room/fact-sheets/detail/adolescent-mental-health[11]

World Health Organization. (2021). Mental health and psychosocial considerations during the COVID-19

---

9. https://www.who.int/mental_health/evidence/en/promoting_mhh.pdf

10. https://www.who.int/docs/default-source/coronaviruse/mental-health-considerations.pdf

11. https://www.who.int/news-room/fact-sheets/detail/adolescent-mental-health

outbreak. Retrieved from https://www.who.int/docs/default-source/coronaviruse/mental-health-considerations.pdf[12]

Wyn, J., Cahill, H., Holdsworth, R., Rowling, L., & Carson, S. (2000). MindMatters, a whole-school approach promoting mental health and wellbeing. *Australian & New Zealand Journal of Psychiatry, 34*(4), 594-601. doi:10.1080/j.1440-1614.2000.00748.x

---

12. https://www.who.int/docs/default-source/coronaviruse/mental-health-considerations.pdf